QUEER COMMUNAL KINSHIP NOW!

Fig. 1. Detail from Hieronymus Bosch, *Ship of Fools* (1490–1500)

First published in 2023 by punctum books, Earth, Milky Way.
https://punctumbooks.com

ISBN-13: 978-1-68571-084-2 (print)
ISBN-13: 978-1-68571-085-9 (ePDF)

DOI: 10.53288/0415.1.00

LCCN: 2023930783
Library of Congress Cataloging Data is available from the Library of Congress

Book design: Vincent W.J. van Gerven Oei

p. punctumbooks

spontaneous acts of scholarly combustion

HIC SVNT MONSTRA

ROBINOU

QUEER COMMUNAL KINSHIP NOW!

p.

CONTENTS

to my kins ❤

A QUEER ENCOUNTER

In August 2019, I stayed nine days sitting on the branches of the weeping willow located at the tip of the Île de la Cité, in Paris. I had already spent extended periods of time in trees as part of my artistic practice, usually in more challenging urban settings. But, at that time, I was going through some chaos in my sentimental life, and therefore was looking for peace and serenity. This calm, idyllic location seemed like the ideal setting to establish my temporary shelter. I was looking for possibilities of experimental relating. Mainly, this tree practice was about encountering fellow urbanites in fugitive, singular, and poetic ways. For this, I was curious to entangle myself with the symbolic and affective charge of that site, widely recognized as one of the most romantic spots of the city.

There is something special about weeping willows, in that their branches, as they shape a sort of curtain that encircles them, create a very intimate space, propitious to romance or melancholy. This particular tree, leaving its long falling branches to rest on the calm water banks of the Seine, isolated at the end of its island, hosted an especially charming atmosphere of softness, as the sun rays gracefully pierced through its leaves that slowly undulated with the wind. As I said, I was in an especially vulnerable and sensitive state of mind. Absorbing the peaceful energy of that place, at the time, felt like a healing process, beyond the inspiration that it provided for my writing. I had a few delightful interactions there, but one has especially and profoundly marked me, and is the reason why I am recalling this story now.

I had been observing people passing by, mostly tourists coming to take pictures of the view, lovers sharing a moment of intimacy, or friends turning up for afterwork drinks. Nourished by this observational state, I had become extra sensitive to the differences and variations in modes of address, in verbal and non-verbal interpersonal communication. Even though certain pairs of lovers were showing particular levels of tenderness, or certain groups of friends a delightful complicity, there was a certain consistency in the demographic I was observing. Even though these people were coming from all different places in the world, I noticed how they mostly related to each other with the same, let's say, constancy and slight rigidity, which kind of contrasted with the serene openness of the place.

In fact, I realized that two factors were prevalent in explaining this phenomenon: first, the gendered nature of their relations. Heterosexual couples constituted the overwhelming majority of my visitors. In many cases, they appeared to act in suspiciously codified manners. Few seemed genuinely happy. In groups of friends, men were often making me feel uncomfortable by the display of their masculinity, manifesting it through higher voice volume and exaggerated or tense body language. Meanwhile, women seemed generally a bit tamer and less invested in their expressivity, as if they had to contain themselves, even when no men were around.

The second factor that really participated in my malaise was the hierarchical relations between parents and children, demonstrating the structural pervasiveness of an oppressive form of kinship. This came out to be the main source of tangible tension and aggression around, as rushed parents coercively pressed children in following their steps or argued with them for various reasons mostly related to the performative gauging of their impregnable authority. Even though the children were them-selves sporadically displaying violent behaviors, it seemed to be much less systematic than the pressure brought on by their su-pervisors. And, in the attitude of the parents, even when things were seemingly going smooth, I could often still perceive what I would best describe as an apprehension of the duty of parent-ing, a sort of tense, permanent state of alert.

Over the course of the week, only one group stood out from all the others: it is about them that I want to share now. When they stepped under the leaf curtain, their entrance produced a complete shift. A groundbreaking, but most peaceful trans-formation, in striking contrast with all my other local human encounters so far — something almost alien. A different type of presence.

A small group of young people, somewhere in this liminal stage between teenage years and adulthood. Coming there for a photoshoot, like many others. What struck me first was the way they were addressing each other verbally: softly, gently, but also clearly, the gaze focused on their interlocutor. Often accompa-nying their words by small physical gestures of affection, almost imperceptible caresses. The smothered atmosphere provided by the willow allowed them to tune down their voices to the most sensitive level and seemed to constitute a perfect match to the affective tonality of their interactions. I remember thinking how no one else had been even remotely acting like them since I was there.

Coming from a somewhat macho culture as a teenager im-mersed within hegemonic masculinity, I wonder if a few years before I would have considered these kids as acting pedantic; but here, no mannerism was involved, simply what I would phrase as a refined culture of sensitivity or attention. There did not seem to be any dissenting tension in their attitudes, and they actually didn't pass to me as gays or lesbians. They sim-ply, seemingly effortlessly were challenging the whole gendered mode of interaction that I had spent a week dissecting and the binary division of gender in which I have framed my story so far. Indeed, they all seemed to address their gendered identity in a less imperative manner, and for some of them, I could not really tell if it was more leaning on one side of the spectrum or the other. Anyway, gender performance seemed mostly irrelevant in their interactions.

They were having a lot of fun, even though their concentration was palpable. Fabio, the photographer, was giving sparse but precise indications while the others were adjusting their outfits and props. We started talking, and I asked them a few questions as I was helping them to set a large veil of sheer fabric in the heights of the tree for their shooting. I was eager to understand from where their tender complicity was coming from. They were not even a group of close friends: half of them had connected through social media a few hours before. In fact, the only thing that united them, in their attitude and discourse, was simple: they were *queer*.

Of course, I am aware of the idealization in my story, and I am also conscious of what is achievable in terms of social interaction at the level of society, compared to the privileged scale of the bubble they seemed to navigate within, the neotribal space of an aesthetically bonding community. But still, there was something profoundly exhilarating and inspirational in the way they related with each other, as breaking out of the scripted and predictable codes of gendered sociability. All my life I had spent in mostly straight spaces. I had been playing and observing that rigid game of heterosexual seduction and competition for so long. On the other hand, gay culture in my social proximity displayed what I took for repulsive traits of mannerism, elitism, and superficiality — I am obviously exposing my own cultural background bias here. This explains why, even though my uninhibited conduct on dance floors has always hinted at my lack of rigid preference in terms of sexual attraction, for a long time I restricted myself to the more sweet and gentle flairs of femininity for my intimacies.

To me, there was a certain level of naivety and shallowness showing through their enterprise. I wondered if they cared about ethics, economic and social justice, or how their lifestyle of narcissistic and libidinal aesthetic daydreaming might be sustained by less privileged individuals. But what they were indisputably doing, by the sheer power of their presence, was to create and promote a different future, one in which people could communicate, express themselves, and relate to each other in more open, fluid, and gentle ways. This encounter really nourished my motivation into carving affective spaces of communal sensitivity and tenderness that are hardly possible to cultivate in heteronormative conditions, as I will attempt to expose in the following pages of this book. This, combined with my interactions with and observations of the tourists, led me to the articulation of aims I wanted to address: first, to deconstruct how gendered dynamics impact the ways we interact between people, impoverishing our sociability; second, to go beyond the possessive and competitive conditionings induced by the norm of the couple; and third, to strike against the tensions of generationality, producing hierarchy and violence in a culture in which generations are framed as conflicting with each other. This is what led me to investigate the social institution that underlies my concerns: the family. This book, as my humble contribution, is my first foray into this territory.

CAPITALISM AND
SOCIAL REPRODUCTION

*Any group which calls itself radical and revolutionary must
concern itself with providing an alternative way for people to
live and work together than the competitive, role-oriented model
which heterosexual, capitalist society offers us.*

— GLF Men's Collective

One ambition of this text is to push for a radical redefinition
of love, intimacy, and care in support of a much-needed redistributive justice movement. This project must be accompanied
by an exit from heteronormativity as a regime of relational scarcity, as well as from the metaphysics of private property which
is at the heart of our economies and, by extension, of our social
ecologies, at odds with much life on this planet. To do this, I
propose to examine the role of western normative family ideals
in the mechanisms of the preservation and intensification of this
status quo, as well as potential approaches to guide us out of this
unsavory situation.

Any project aiming to deconstruct the family would be well
advised to seek guidance in the writings of Gilles Deleuze and
Félix Guattari, in particular their *Anti-Oedipus: Capitalism and*

Schizophrenia from 1972. In this book, they develop a conceptual framework which provides us with crucial tools to grasp the type of relationship between desire and capital, or the power arrangements that combine social exploitation and psychological repression.

In his introduction to the English edition of the book, Mark Seem clearly synthesizes the authors' stated goal in *Anti-Oedipus*: to initiate a radical politics of desire freed from all beliefs. To do so, "[t]hey urge mankind to strip itself of all anthropomorphic and anthropological armoring, all myth and tragedy, and all existentialism, in order to perceive what is nonhuman in man, his will and his forces, his transformations and mutations" (Deleuze and Guattari 2009, xvii).

Indeed, this is Deleuze and Guattari's central thesis: the societal organization of relational patterns that orient the flows of desire in a capitalist economy is sustained by the systemic naturalization of a theater of the unconscious, where Oedipus is the figurehead of imperialism, the bedrock of a narrative construction haunted by its role in a patriarchal-colonial history of domination and uniformization.

Thus it is good to recall, as Seem does, that "[d]epression and Oedipus are agencies of the State, agencies of paranoia, agencies of power, long before being delegated to the family" (xx). This is indeed where the link between capitalism and patriarchy operates, in the way the two systems feed each other in *intra-action* (Barad 2007), by the spreading of ideologically induced, cognitive logics applied at the level of the economy and internalized by the individual based on a metaphysics of hierarchy (essentialism), distinction (individualism), and exclusion (privatism). Through this ideological apparatus, the family as an institution is essential to forming class divisions and handing them down from generation to generation (Barrett and McIntosh 2015, 155).

One of the conceptual propositions I would like to put forward in this text is a framework in which patriarchy is investigated as an economic system and capitalism as a symbiotic formation of that patriarchal order. Patriarchy is indeed, if more than anything, an economic system, one of transmission, re-production, and authority. As the basic principle required by a capitalist articulation of the world, private property is the insti-tution that makes patriarchy reproduce itself, through symbolic and material appropriations.

There is no doubt that the hegemony of the capitalist system is driving us toward major desolation in every ecological di-mension of existence, in the social, psychic, and environmental realms (Guattari 2014). Therefore, it might be necessary to stir the discussion about abolishing private property, not in an ab-solute sense but as the systematic conditioning of our relational practices. The angle of this book will be to initiate this enter-prise with a problematization of the western patriarchal family in order to derail its reproduction by proposing an alternative conceptual apparatus.

My postulate is therefore the following: the poverty and the sadness of our relational landscape today are reinforced by the dominance of a subjectivity dictated by the codes of neoliberal capitalism. This phenomenon largely relies on the social forma-tion of the bourgeois family, as it has naturalized itself as a dom-inant model over the last centuries. Precisely, I will attempt to show that what lies behind British Deputy Prime Minister John Prescott's 1997 declaration that "we're all middle-class now" is a familialist ideology, which, through the enforcement of middle-class as the default subjective position, fed the fantasized iden-tification to a societal order obedient to the tragic governance of capital.

In their work, Deleuze and Guattari develop an anti-oedipal resistance force, a revolutionary collective of orphans (no dad-dy–mommy–me), atheists (no beliefs), and nomads (no habits, no territories). One of the approaches of this book will be to update and refine the traits of the conceptual characters neces-sary to the imagination of a society emancipated from the codes of a naturalized bourgeoisie by uniting them in the unique but nevertheless polymorphous figure of the queer. Queer theory, stemming from a long tradition that goes back to our post-

structuralist forebears and arising from the rhizomatic extensions of feminist thought, provides in this framework its heroic
figure as an agent of radical denaturalization. I propose to focus
on the matter of queering social reproduction and to start with
the following questions: how can queerness be perpetuated by
constructing the conditions that make its reproduction possible
and legitimate? How can we defend the notion of queer kinship
as a political necessity, a strategy of transmission, a post-familial
praxis for the twenty-first century? Finally, how can we sustain
alternative pathways to the individualist and consumerist, normalizing tendencies striking among queer communities?

In order to sketch out answers to these complex questions,
I found it necessary to move away from a rigorously scientific
approach so as to conceive a conceptual framework of social
reproduction capable of emancipating its agents from familialist constraints. In its speculative dimension, this proposal can
therefore be located in the realm of anticipatory or utopian writing. Social theory that invokes the concept of utopia has always
been vulnerable to charges of naivety, impracticality, or lack of
rigor. But, as José Esteban Muñoz reminds us in his book *Cruising Utopia,* one of the texts with which I will expand my definition of queerness in this book: "Hope as an hermeneutic [...]
is nothing short of necessary in order to combat the force of
political pessimism" (Muñoz 2009, 4). Therefore, my conceptual
articulation borrows both from the codes of literature and social science in order to shift the ruts of our perception of reality
through the exercise of a problematization, that of the bourgeois
family.

Confronted with the metaphysics of individualism, competition, and property which permeate western philosophy, scientific theories that naturalize the bourgeois family, a brutal and
inegalitarian culture that reproduces itself incessantly, and the
necessary upheaval of what is called *common sense,* it is urgent
to theorize a framework of emancipation that integrates the
question of (social) reproduction. Imagining a new conception
of family is therefore a necessarily transgressive political project
in that it must summon an ethical rigor absent from the struc-

tures of social reproduction in which we have grown up. This book is not presented as an instruction manual or a procedure to follow but rather as a set of tools for the elaboration of emancipatory stories, new narratives of belonging.

The heteropatriarchal family nourishes the cognitive biases that fracture the social fabric, the economic logics that exhaust the material world. To denaturalize the bourgeois family will require the decolonization of the subconscious and the re-eroticization of the world. This is what will be attempted in this text, notably through a fundamental questioning of the notion of the romantic couple. Bringing a child into the world within the exclusive, possessive, and emotionally unstable framework of the libidinal relationship between two individuals, given the tools of thought available to us today, should appear as a systemic aberration and a form of child abuse to anyone who can boast of the ambition of a better world.

Denaturalizing the couple, romantic love, and modes of family organization centered around biogenetic reproduction are a series of most exciting challenges because they completely overturn some of our cultural codes and open the way to fairer, more open, and more cheerful forms of social organization. They are also challenges that must be tackled urgently because these normative rigidities deftly but inflexibly reduce our field of possibilities by their imposition of desensitized relations. On the contrary, the reader can only rejoice at the perspective that these pages attempt to draw: a convivial, accessible mode of affective relationality, freed from its humanistic, anthropocentric, and heteronormative shackles. It is a matter of developing this mode well.

Whereas *Anti-Oedipus* was intended to be a work revolting against simplicity, which by its hydra-like form and baroque nuances resists the sirens of synthesis and gracefully takes us to the sublime of abstraction, my ambition is lighter and perhaps also less ambitious: that of attempting to consolidate different discourses into one narrative, providing the reader with a panorama hopefully stimulating their own thought process on a cultural phenomenon, in this case, the family. In that sense, this book is an exercise in diffractive reading, navigating around sources from the anarchist, communist, and feminist traditions, brought together through the prism of a queer sensitivity. It is more of a dance in a field rather than the majestic creation of concepts which is what, for Deleuze and Guattari, defined the practice of philosophy. Here, it is more a matter of consolidating a story by drifting critically through conceptual landscapes already present in the social. This book is to be comprehended as a mobilizing piece, so much of the conceptual depth of its remarks will remain limited by its concern for impact, that of a direct address: it is time to change our relational habits. We don't know what we are capable of.

In the first chapter, "The Hegemonic Family," I will look at the historical evidence for the correlation between capitalism and patriarchy in the consolidation of the bourgeois model of the nuclear family. I dive into the material, structural, and power dynamics that elevated that model throughout the last centuries to the point of its current hegemonic status in the west. Through a genealogical approach, I shape a conceptualization of the normative family as a political and economic, agentive pattern integrated within the logics of patriarchal capitalism. This is not a rigorous attempt at vulgarization but, instead, a rough overview of the topic. It could also be distilled into the axiom that, while our traditional family model is nowadays challenged in many ways, it remains a pervasive force on our collective imagination of the social.

In the second chapter, "Resistance and Contestation," I will look at the controversies around the family that have emerged in our recent history, and alternatives developed in some politicized circles of our contemporary societies. I focus on forms of social organization that occur and develop outside of or in reaction to the hetero-patriarcal family, articulating this through three different axes: the family as a privatized system of household-based social reproduction, the couple-form, and the privileging of biogenetic-centered kinship. I then look into different contemporary relational frameworks that challenge this normative model and uncover their potential as well as their limitations.

Hopefully, these investigations will inform the project of the third chapter, "Queer Communal Kinship," which is to conceptualize an emancipated form of social reproduction organized around the notion of *queer communal kinship,* forging a proposition that requires the enthusiasm and openness of *queer,* the pragmatic and organizational aspects of *communal,* and the denaturalized imaginative focus of *kinship.* This speculative model will serve as the conceptual apparatus to elaborate alternative approaches to the inegalitarian and closed relational logics of patriarchal capitalism.

As an author engaged in critical discourse, I face a certain tension between the transparent disclosure of my position of enunciation and my right to discretion. In what follows, I will succinctly attempt to comply with my duty while negotiating this delicate balance. It is important to situate this impulsive text, written in ten months at the height of the pandemic, as the product of a young queer-in-becoming. It is therefore tinted with frustration and fear but also the exhilarating feeling of engaging myself on a truly emancipatory pathway.

Evidently, I am very much the product of what I denounce, having been born among self-righteous, middle-class, non-intellectual families strongly inclined toward maintaining their privileged position in the social order. On my father's side, this came with a strong emphasis on reproduction and competition. My father has three brothers, and they all have three children. The petty bourgeois family's motto: in life, you can choose whatever path you like, but there is one rule, you have to be the best. Talk about realistic goals. No need to mention that my cousins are all either studying law, medicine, or engineering. On my mother's father's side, it's a different narrative, one of social ascent in the spirit of the golden 1950s: the story of brave working-class people, my great-grandparents, sacrificing their lives to allow their children to climb the social ladder, providing space to my grandpa, a goodwilled but uneducated nouveau riche who offered his life to corporate interests in order to afford himself some level of mostly performative wealth.

I'm skipping less relevant details. The point is, I'm a white, middle-class kid, and I am afraid that what you have in hand is little more than middle-class literature. Sorry, you won't find any sharp working-class or intersectional analysis here. Furthermore, my repeated use of the abstraction "the west" — I skipped the capitalization, in order not to sacralize it — simply means that I have no clue what's happening outside that space and wouldn't pretend to give any advice to those I never met, even though the history of western imperialism means that the cultural issues I'm addressing in this book might resonate elsewhere. Similarly, there are certainly queer lives lived in the countryside, but that is again beyond the scope of this book. Mainly, I write with my direct social environment in mind: young, urban Europeans reaching an age where the notions of kinship and social reproduction become part of their questionings. Yes, I do this self-centered thing of doing research for myself, I hope you don't mind.

Regarding my gender identity, I alternate between fluid, queer, non-binary, and trans (update one year later: I'm now a full-grown transfem queen yas!), even though I try not to hide the fact that I grew up as one of them, the males, the oppressors, the predators, those you cannot trust when you've grown up in a world that objectifies, sexualizes, and weakens you. My trajectory through feminism and queerness came late, and in a sense I feel legitimate to talk about deconstruction since I have for long experienced what hegemonic, masculine subjectivity feels like. On some levels, it is kind of surreal to look back. I have come a long way and embarked on this journey, thanks to a privileged, feminist environment but mostly through my own, deliberate quest for emancipation through intellectual work, spending weeks in libraries, studying the canons of feminist and queer theory. The material conditions that supported this process, my privileges in terms of financial independence, cannot be overlooked.

Still, I am bitter at how long I conformed to society's heteronormative codes. While I can confidently say today that I am bi or pansexual, I still sometimes notice in me subtle, latent traces of homophobia, remnants of my teenage socialization in the macho, urban culture of the South of France. Homophobia is less the aversion to gay people than it is to one's own desires. It took me a while to understand this. In retrospect, I definitely have missed out on a certain lightness in my youth and didn't have the chance to explore some of my queer desires. So, in a way, I'm writing for my younger self and hope that my work might benefit those who, like me, got trapped in the dead-ends of normative gender and sexuality.

To summarize, I have been socialized as a man and conceived of myself as cishet until my mid-twenties. I have been living in many different shared houses for the last decade but not always by choice. I have been experimenting with polyamory and relationship anarchy for a few years, not always without trouble. And, finally, I'm not closely involved in the education of children. So, I'm not pretending to have an extensive experience of queerness, communal living, nor kinship. This book is not an ethnography of queer families or queer communal living. It is also not a straightforward guide into ethical relationships of bonding. Mainly I'm interested in philosophy and literature as subjectivity-shifting tools, supporting the cognitive reprogramming that emancipates us from normative thinking. In that sense, my contribution with this book is simply to incentivize its reader to make this kind of mental displacement: to think less about family, and more about queer communal kinship, as concepts to imagine different worlds. Let's go!

I

THE HEGEMONIC FAMILY

*Caring, sharing and loving would be more widespread if the
family did not claim them for its own.*
— Barrett and McIntosh (1991, 82)

In this chapter, I loosely follow Michel Foucault's notion of genealogy as a sort of exercise in exposing and tracing the installa-
tion and operation of false universals. Through this approach, I
want to shape a conceptualization of the bourgeois family as an
economic institution, with capitalism as one of its origins and
reinforcing factors. I conclude with an account of the intricacies
between the nuclear family and capital, with a special focus on
accumulation, and how the dominance of the normative family model takes part in the most violent and unequal aspects of
our current economic system, in line with the insensitivity of a
subject shaped by its neoliberal environment.

1. Naturalization

First, I want to present our family organization model for what
it is: a cultural, historical construct. I then want to expose the
current implications of this particular arrangement by identify-

ing the psychosocial patterns naturalized by the bourgeois family that are in confluence with a capitalist regime of desire.

sexuality

In his essay "Is There a History of Sexuality?" David M. Halperin (1989) traces the origins of the concept of sexuality and locates them in the era of modernity. Indeed, what this concise essay unravels is "sexuality" as a cultural product: it represents the appropriation of the human body and of its physiological capacities by an ideological discourse. It is always a good idea to repeat this as it may seem counterintuitive to someone raised in postmodern times: sexuality is a modern concept. Same thing goes for the categories of heterosexuality or homosexuality. These terms didn't exist prior to modernity, and they are simply cultural artifacts, tools of historically situated discourse, but through their existence as material semiotics, they're also shaping our understanding of the real. As Halperin emphasizes, it is his work as historian to reveal the purely conventional and arbitrary character of our own social and sexual identities.

This is thus a good reminder that constitutive cultural notions necessarily become naturalized through time. That means that they "patch" themselves onto what was previously considered as "nature"; for example, the schemas of romantic love are nowadays often conflated with biological mechanisms of human reproduction for the simple reason that bio-genetic reproduction has long been the only conceivable way of reproduction for our species. The belief that this mode of reproduction has anything more "natural" than others, including those that are yet-to-come, relies on an old nature-versus-culture dichotomy that has long been dispelled by feminist theory.

In his essay, Halperin argues for "a new, and radical, historical sociology of psychology, an intellectual discipline designed to analyze the cultural poetics of desire, by which I mean the processes whereby sexual desires are constructed, mass-produced, and distributed among the various members of human living-groups" (273). This discourse evidently recalls the thesis of *Anti-Oedipus,* that the social field is the historically determined product of desire, where "desire produces the real" (Deleuze and Guattari 2009, 35).

Thus, what Halperin urges us is to "train ourselves to recognize conventions of feeling as well as conventions of behavior and to interpret the intricate texture of personal life as an artifact, as the determinate outcome, of a complex and arbitrary constellation of cultural processes" (Halperin 1989, 273). I want to examine the model of the bourgeois family and how it has been raised to its hegemonic status as socio-cultural construction. A brief, genealogical account will unveil the naturalization process through which the kinship organization of a very specific culture that some even call a weird one — western, educated, industrialized, rich, and democratic — has become a strong imperial model in a globalized world. I believe this model produces relational patterns of miserable quality, a major source of sadness around the globe.

Grief in the Nuclear Model

Let's turn to bourgeois grief. Those like me who have western, middle-class culture as their living environment will certainly share the agonizing memory of having participated in the funeral of an elderly person whose partner was still alive. Beyond the terrifying standardized ritual of the funeral ceremony, an archetypal staging of the bourgeoisie with its speeches and honors, what strikes with the most clarity is the miserable relational condition in which the unfortunate widow or widower often finds themselves.

Even surrounded in the best of cases by an extended family network or strong friendships, the survivor is then cut off from their primary relationship, the one around which their entire existence has been built. Indeed, common stories depict men who could not survive more than a few weeks after their wives passed away (Creamer 2011), and widows who could not envisage finding another companion after their husband left. The end of life within a nuclear family model is often an experience of isolation, which comes after an equally terrible imprisonment in the patriarchal routine of the aging couple. This sad relational pattern, the ironic fate of a privileged group of individuals who, by their excessive accumulation of wealth, destroy the living conditions of those they exploit, can be explained by the generalization of a cultural norm that has been pushed way, way too far: that of the couple.

In the context of this mode of mourning, it is interesting to look at its epistemological dimension and to see how psychoanalytical science itself naturalizes a normative conception of the family based on the bourgeois model. Indeed, when understood as a linear, predictable process, the script that follows the common understanding of the psychology of grief — the one that is taught in western universities — naturalizes bourgeois grief, since it's been developed exclusively on the basis of observations taken from that specific relational model.

This example of grief, or the isolation produced by our normative model of family, is only one indication of a larger trend in western relational patterns, the illustration of an underlying cultural attitude, one of *toxic indifference*. What we observe in individualistic consumerist society is a crisis of care and solidarity, one that leads us to increased loneliness and depression, not to speak about ecological disaster. To take a recent reference, the west's handling of the Covid-19 pandemic of 2020 is striking in how it has revealed the extent of that indifference, giving us an idea of the stage of our civilization's decadence.

In choosing a relatable event, the death of an elder, I try to raise the following question: if we have no sensitivity to the misery of the people next to us, if we're only sad about the event but doing nothing to change its structural causes, how are we even going to address the modern slavery produced by our consumerist and segregationist obsessions? Are we going to continue to, at best, feel bad about it, but do nothing? Luckily, the example of grief also raises the specific matter to address in order, perhaps, to start solving this issue, the one of selective care exemplified in the normative generationality of the bourgeois family.

The Metaphysics of the Bloodline

In the bloodline we find a common and founding principle of patriarchy and capitalism: accumulation. For this we have to dive into a psychological consideration of the patrilineal mechanism of transmission. It is fairly easy to understand that most men, when they reach a certain age, become afraid of death — when I refer to "men," I'm talking about individuals who have internalized the values and cultural roles associated with masculinity. In a desperate attempt to transcend the inescapable, a common psychological mechanism they deploy is to project onto their children the continuation of their success, of their actions that are sacralized by normative cultural validation. This is the ground of selective care that excludes extended and ecological considerations, in favor of the private interests of the lineage through symbolic and economic accumulation. This is another job for the queer psychology researcher, that is, *how to teach men how to die.* Unfortunately, this would require at least a different study, if not a whole career. Nonetheless, maybe the simplest way is to let men stop being men, eventually. This may only happen, I would argue, in an alternative framework to the patriarchal family, a context we need to build and advocate for, in order for it to ultimately become legible.

To understand the mechanism of transmission happening with patriarchy, we need to focus our attention on the abstraction of the bloodline. Indeed, nowadays many people still believe in this mystical biological connection that only serves the agenda of conservative, exclusionary, and inequitable politics. Commercially speaking, it is impressive to see how the metaphysics of blood filiation is commodified by online genealogy platforms by reaching aimless elders whose entire existence is centered around that accomplished narrative, with grandchildren as their most tangible achievement and the last meaningful justification of their existence.

Blood carries centuries of poisonous metaphors. Ironically, one of the fathers of capitalism, Adam Smith, was already conscious of this when he wrote his *Theory of Moral Sentiments*:

"This force of blood [...] exists nowhere but in tragedies and romances. [...] To imagine any such mysterious affection [...] would be ridiculous" (1759, 261). Nevertheless, in his days, this narrative of the bloodline supported the interests of the family as the main political and economic institution of its time: it's important to note that in colonial America, two-thirds of elected politicians had kinship ties to other politicians, and the corporation hadn't yet replaced the family business (D.S. Smith 1993, 344). So, what we find is that this dynamic of accumulation concentrated inside the family produces patterns of competition, distancing, and exclusion. If corporations have replaced the family business as the structural economic agent, the commercial logic of patriarchy never left the family house. It just displaced itself into the symbolic order of success evaluated by wealth and the continuation of the bloodline.

2. Genealogy

It's not my ambition of to retrace the history of the western family through the ages. Indeed, expert scholars have done that in the past, and it would be dangerously simplistic for me to try to summarize such a complex history. What I want to do is to briefly look at some key landmarks of the naturalization of this modern family. While it is tempting to go back to our good old imperial Roman ancestors to try to locate the sources of our patriarchal tradition, I want to limit my analysis to a few specific historical observations from modernity that, taken all together, unwrap the imposition and consequent universalization of the bourgeois nuclear family through our recent history or shed light on how this process went mostly uncompromised.

The church

A major factor in the enforcement of the nuclear family model in western history has been the influence of the church, as one of the earlier, premodern historical institutions that played seriously with what Foucault famously termed biopolitics. Concretely, in France, the history of civil status has its roots in the practices of the catholic church. The clergy participates in the organization of births and encourages the formation of normalized households. Most generally, the connection between christianity, especially protestantism, and the individualistic or nuclear tendencies of the European family system is a thoroughly analyzed historical phenomenon. More broadly, the conservatism of most religious institutions, with regard to family in the west, is to be found in the axiom of all monotheistic religions, namely, the sacred nature of human life and procreation (Braidotti 2008, 10). The moralist position regarding the evolution of our bio-technological practices seals the heteronormative family as the only conceivable kinship formation for the conservative value system of these patriarchal institutions.

The Bourgeois Model

The bourgeois family model, before its imposition as the most widespread cultural ideal in western society, was primarily rooted in the ruling classes of the European eighteenth century (Berger and Berger 1983). This premodern family model moves in modernity to what we call the "nuclear family": parents living together and sharing responsibility for their children and for each other. In addition to being nuclear, the bourgeois family is structured around the following characteristics: a strictly gendered distribution of roles; an emphasis on normative moral standards, especially with regard to sexuality; a profound interest in the welfare of children, especially their proper education; and the inculcation of values and attitudes conducive to economic success and personal responsibility. The cultural hegemony of this model led to its progressive naturalization in our culture. Nowadays the term "bourgeois" has lost its relevance since it references a specific historical class, also called "Victorian" in England or "middle class" in the US. Nonetheless, the repercussions of the bourgeois model of family are very much present in our contemporary culture.

universalism

Another way the family got naturalized is by the tendency of old, white men to think that whatever they experience in their comfortable reality should represent universal truths. We can go back to 1762 with Jean-Jacques Rousseau to see how this principle of the family as an indisputable and primarily natural institution is at the root of western modern philosophy. For him, the family is "the oldest of all societies, and the only natural one" (1999, 46). This principle is also exemplified, two centuries later, in the Universal Declaration of Human Rights, for which "[t]he family is the natural and fundamental group unit of society and is entitled to protection by society and the State" (UN General Assembly 1948). These two major documents show well how modernity has erected the modern family as a cosmological truth. Unfortunately, this is not without its victims: feminist critique is well equipped to show how universalism masks inequalities (MacKinnon 2007).

colonization

It is important to note that the modern, western family is inscribed in a history of violence. It has not evolved organically to reach its current hegemonic status but has been repeatedly enforced throughout history. The most evident way to illustrate that fact is to look back at our colonial past. Indeed, historians have shown how African kin networks were destroyed under slavery (Freeman 2008, 303). Especially relevant to our thesis is the historical episode in post-slavery America when African Americans were forced to comply with the heteronuclear model of family in order to qualify for the entitlements of full citizenship (Franke 2013). That imposed model of the American, white family culminated in the decades of rapid change in the household after World War II (D.S. Smith 1993, 343), that led to the establishment of the nuclear family as the only legible form of kinship formation from the 1950s onward in the US.

We need to take into consideration the consequences of a culture defined by its dominant position in the geopolitical power relations of the colonial era in order to answer the following questions: what does it mean to grow up in a world in which important aspects of your material reality are sustained by the exploitation of distant resources and labor? How does this impact the way individuals construct themselves psychologically and position themselves in a collective, or with regard to ecology?

There are no doubts that the currently dominant, western family model is intrinsically linked with our colonial history. One could say that imperialism is patterned on the paternalist and exclusive model of the traditional western family with its logics of expansion and competition. This was the case, for example, when the "Orient" was feminized in western literature as a land to be metaphorically "penetrated," that is, invaded by the patriarchal figure of the white savior (Said 1978, 211). As a rhetoric, colonialism has always been linked with the most abject paternalism. Therefore, it is of major relevance today to consider the cultural implications of the fact that our family model consolidated itself in a context of colonial expropriation over centuries. Colonialism is our culture and is ingrained in the shapes of our social organization, in which our family model is maybe the most conservative and lingering institution.

Another issue is the appropriation of labor for the needs of the patriarchal family. With regard to this historical context, it is important to emphasize that the ideal image of the white bourgeois family as a happy, self-sufficient entity is an entirely artificial construct. There have always been marginalized others taking part in its reproduction. Today, the lifestyle of western privileged families could not be maintained without the hidden intervention of racialized and sexualized, locally and globally outsourced labor. This is nothing new: it is how the nuclear family model has been sustained, in the US at least, since the plantations.

The second wave

Relative to a historical overview of the consolidation of the western hegemonic family model, it also seems important to focus on certain episodes that may explain the inability of counterforces to oppose this model. As a movement that confronts the order of patriarchal power, feminism is the most obvious candidate when it comes to emblematizing this force of resistance. Notably, Sabine Fortino (1997) has set out to explain why reproduction has long been an unthought aspect of the feminist movement. By analyzing texts produced during what is now called the "second feminist wave," she puts her finger on one of the reasons that can explain the relative reserve of feminist interests when it comes to questioning the issues of parenthood and filiation.

At the height of its dynamism at the end of the 1960s, the feminist movement in France was vividly engaged in the struggle for access and the right to abortion, a struggle that at the time was of major political importance (women must be able to have control over their bodies) and an important social issue (children abandoned to public assistance) and thus catalyzed much of the energy deployed in speeches and actions. Therefore, this crystallization of the debates around unwanted motherhood may explain the lack of discursive engagement around that which is desired (4).

Moreover, Fortino notes that during the consolidation of second feminist wave, the utopia of a radical emancipation of female roles developed, in which motherhood is conceived as a kind of slavery, a coerced obedience to the traditional role of the woman–mother, linking the reproductive role and domestic work. This discourse was consolidated by the homogeneity of the social composition of the movement, mainly consisting of young unmarried and childless women. Fortino notes that it was not until a few years later, the years 1976 to 1978, that the preoccupation with motherhood emerged in the discursive field of feminism, as evidenced by the various publications devoted to it at the time. These discourses then re-naturalized the essentialism of motherhood by emphasizing its "natural" or biological nature and thus in itself legitimate as a practice of a strong and emancipated femininity.

The Fall of Socialism

The socialist utopian vision of fostering greater social justice by integrating women into the work sphere put considerable pressure on traditional conceptions of the family. At the time of the Soviet Union, countries in Eastern Europe were pioneering in providing support for families and children as well as educational and medical services that surpassed preceding models in bourgeois societies (Hering 2009). The transition toward capitalism is an interesting historical episode to look at since with it came the progressive imposition of the bourgeois family model, with man as provider and woman as caretaker, which was relatively absent under socialism (Gapova 2016, 15).

In the 1990s, as socialism was "substituted" with capitalism and liberal democracy with their emphasis on individual autonomy and responsibility for one's own well-being, the welfare systems were largely dismantled, and functions formerly delegated to the public domain were reassigned to the private sphere. The brief period of celebration of newly acquired freedoms was subsequently followed by a recognition that women, the elderly, and people with disabilities were losing under the free market. The fall of the communist bloc, as a key moment of consolidation for the global capitalist hegemony, consequently coincided with the privatization of the social that was detrimental to those who did not fit into the normative model of the bourgeois family.

Capitalism

One of the principles of capitalism is that it is an economic system in which the free market creates competition between different actors and that this dynamic generates innovation as well as opportunities for all — a vision idealized in the model of the American dream, personified by the self-made man in a sort of

Darwinian narrative—a dialectical pirouette in which the law of the strongest is erected as a model of emancipation by a certain conception of liberalism that could certainly be described as naïve or at least superficial. This narrative unfolding is mirrored in the transposition of the theory of natural selection to the evolution of human societies, a transposition that has been used to justify the orchestrated annihilation of any form of social organization other than that proper to western modernity. This evolutionary approach to culture—that is, the inscription in the ideological perspective of a progressive evolution of human societies—naturalizes the principle of competition between different societal models. This discourse simply has the unspoken aim of preserving the properties of western history by stating them in the sense of progress, with the heteronormative family as the ultimate realization of human essence at the heart of this apparatus.

Thus, the nuclear and heteronormative family has been consolidated on the ideological bases of an understanding of reality conditioned by a predatorial state of competition, even though it is immensely reductive of evolutionary dynamics. Just as the Oedipal myth constrains the psychoanalytic framework in a mythological theater of the unconscious, social Darwinism eclipses the multiple realities of the organization of the living, in effect eliminating, for example, symbiotic narratives in favor of a predation and competition scheme. Quite the opposite, it is through a dynamic of symbiosis between capitalism and the bourgeois family, exemplified in the historical period of the family-as-business that preceded the emergence of corporations, that we see the consolidation of a competitive mentality between the different actors of the social field and of a public–private distinction consecrating the family as an exclusive and privileged space for the accumulation of capital. Indeed, it is when the European bourgeoisie assumed class dominance over the aristocracy and proletariat in the eighteenth and nineteenth centuries that this binary separation of social spheres annexed middle-class women to the home, leaving the realm of politics and commerce to men (McHugh 1999)—an instance in which capitalism and patriarchy are basically indistinguishable from one another.

Neoliberalism

If anything, neoliberalism exacerbates the mechanisms at stake in previous stages of capitalist expansion: fragmentation of the social, fluidization and acceleration of the circulation of goods and people, intensification of the commodification, and assimilation processes through which every aspect of the social becomes capitalized. In this context, the illusion of choice that characterizes neoliberal subjectivity finds its perfect illustration with the normative model of the family, with political forces hiding their assimilationist agendas by deploying liberal discourses of inclusivity, while also refuting any agency for movements defending real alternatives to this conservative view of society.

In terms of relational practices in regard to the family, the neoliberal agenda has enforced what could be described as a privatization or "home-ification" of care (Silverstein 2020, 8), relocating reproductive responsibility from the state to families and communities to reduce government spending. This, together with the permanent state of emergency prevalent in contemporary political discourse and media affects (Klein 2008), can reinforce a withdrawal into the household, accompanied with a rising attachment towards conservative family values. This conservatism extends by capillarity to other social institutions, when societal values naturalized by the traditional family model are plated on other dimensions of the social organization.

The conception of family as conflated with the notion of home, as a safe space ultimately synonymous with the idea of privacy, takes part in a dynamic that maintains a spatial organization of the social articulated around a sexual dichotomy: because women are so often associated with family, home space becomes seen as a private, feminized space that is distinct from the public, masculinized space that lies outside of its borders (Collins 1998, 67). This unequal symbolic distribution of space is itself responsible for reinforcing gendered inequalities, from the psychosocial violence inflicted on women in their use of public space, most especially in urban areas, to their persistent subordination to men in employment and politics. This phenomenon is only one of the many manifestations of the mechanism by which the family produces real segregated spaces based on a symbolic mapping, much like nations, as that is what hides behind the dual meaning of "domestic" as both residential dwelling and national territory.

Indeed, another way in which our family model permeates society is in the public policies of all sorts that link family and nation, exemplified conceptually in the historical similarities between processes of adopting children and of acquiring citizenship, both processes of "naturalization" that are patterned on the model of the reproductive family, making the child/citizen legally indistinguishable from a biological or native one. In many instances, social security systems around the western world are structurally inspired by the model of the reproductive family, further naturalized by its inscription into our social institutions. Think, for example, of the many contemporary ramifications of the Roman law notion of *bonus pater familias* or good family father.

neo-feudalism

In their book *Le genre du capital,* Céline Bessière and Sybille Gollac argue that in the twenty-first century, family economic capital has once again become central to the construction of the social status of individuals. By developing a materialist sociology of the family institution and focusing specifically on patrimony and heritage, they show how the family, which they suggest we consider as an economic institution in its own right, is a major obstacle to a fairer redistribution of resources in that it contributes to maintaining class boundaries and to deepening economic inequalities between men and women.

They highlight economic tendencies which, by the fact that they seem to be in a phase of consolidation, should alarm us about the urgent need to develop alternatives and deviant discourses in the face of the normative family model. Wealth inequality, which economists thought was destined to be reduced with the rise of the wage society in the twentieth century, has been increasing over the last three decades. It is more and more difficult for an individual without inheritance to climb the economic ladder by relying solely on the income from their work. This phenomenon is accompanied by a steadily increasing wealth gap between men and women, which in France rose from 9 percent in 1998 to 16 percent in 2015 (Bessière and Gollac 2020, 15).

These tendencies reveal what I would qualify as a neo-feudal direction taken by western societies, with a clear intensification of class stratification and a centralization of the modes of subject production by cognitive capitalism (de Boever and Neidich 2013; Moulier Boutang 2011) or what Julien Assange calls high tech liberalism (Southbank Centre 2015), and an increasing reliance on necropolitical strategies by national, supranational, and corporate agencies.

Concretely, the implication of our family model in this dynamic, resulting from the myriad of political decisions that favored the economic development of normative families throughout our civilization, can be pinpointed in the considerable rise in valuation of real estate in central parts of the western world, leading to an increasing economic polarization in which a precarious section of society is economically subordinated to real estate owners (Christophers 2020). This class of landlords, for whom ownership functions as a financial asset and a private system of retirement, can be seen as neo-colonial and anti-queer in the sense that it finds its historical provenance in the wealth of local families and corporations, thus disadvantaging immigrants and individuals diverging from the normative family ideal.

In this context, ownership of a residence is very much a condition for economic stability, and this ownership is very much conditioned by two things: the transmission of wealth operated within the family or the compliance with heteronormative standards in order to acquire such property. This is why the traditional family ideal shows the family not only occupying a home but owning it (Collins 1998, 73). Therefore, in our period of austerity politics and continuing destruction of the social welfare state operated by neoliberal powers, it is easy to formulate the hypothesis that a strengthening of family values — or more precisely a polarization between people who adhere to them or not — can be expected: if one cleaves to the rules of marriage and childbearing, wealth is directly transferable from generation to generation, and this process is increasingly determinant in securing a decent existence.

Instrumental Familialism

It seems appropriate to close this section with a word about the family in its pure ideological form, that is, when it is elevated to the rank of the sacred in a rhetoric that goes beyond biological or moral arguments and establishes it as the pillar of the social order. This familialist discourse deployed in particular by western religious authorities is complemented by the evolutionary rhetoric previously mentioned, which classifies civilizations on the basis of a social Darwinism that sees the evolution of human societies as ordered in a progressive vision leading to its most accomplished form: the modern western society organized around its family model.

In France, this is notably the position articulated by the supporters of the *Manif pour tous,* a collective of mostly catholic associations opposing the law opening marriage and adoption to same-sex couples in 2013 (Dejeans 2017). This major media event in French political life also reveals another instrumental dimension of the family model if we follow the hypothesis developed by Éric Fassin (2015b), a sociologist who specialized in the evolution of the family in France. According to him, the fact that right-wing parties have seized upon the issue of marriage for all to criticize the socialist party governance can be explained by the fact that the latter mobilizes a political program that is not very different from their own.

In fact, marriage for all, in that it was the main banner of the left during this period, allowed the economic or migratory stakes to be eclipsed, which could have revealed the little ideological gap remaining between the so-called left and right parties rallied to the same neoliberal agenda. Thus, in its instrumentalization as a political cause, and even when it is summoned by supposedly progressive and inclusive discourses, the family in fact serves as a smokescreen for the conservatism of political parties that are supposed to defend the positions of citizens with whom certain so-called "left-wing" aspirations persist.

3. conclusion

Today, the family model that shapes our organization of the social, as its most crystallized structural element, is the result of its modern history of entanglement within colonial, patriarchal, and capitalist formations. It is wading in the universalizing assumptions of post-Enlightenment secular liberalism, stuck in the linear logic of progress, corrupted by logics of competition, accumulation, and hierarchy. Even though that model is currently crumbling at an accelerated pace, many of us still rely partly on its idealized form to imagine our life trajectories and define our aspirations. Especially in moments of distress, the fantasy of normative relationships often maintains itself as the only projected haven from the daily insecurities of contemporary existence.

The idea of denaturalizing this institution of social reproduction is to say that no matter what came before, it is possible to invent something completely different from what we are doing now. It is a resistance to felonious traditions, a constructive way of saying fuck habits that reproduce sadness, suffering, and inequality. This work can only be fruitful if it is nourished by a study of the forms of resistance that have been developed in recent history, with a particular focus on the discourses and concepts on which they relied. This will be the subject of the next chapter.

II

RESISTANCE AND CONTESTATION

*It is a matter, I am not saying to rediscover, but to manufacture
other forms of pleasures, relationships, coexistences, links, loves,
intensities.*

— Foucault (1994, 261)

The critique of the nuclear family has always been in tension
with the problem of conceptualizing what could replace it as a
social institution. Notably, conservative voices never miss their
chance to emphasize the recurrent failure of communes to provide a sustaining alternative, or the benefits for the children of
heterosexual couples over single parent households. Indeed, recent research in psychological development (Luyten et al. 2010)
has established that children do need the consistent attention
of a small number of adults early in life, in opposition to some
historical, radical feminist discourses that have mistakenly seen
mother–infant bonds as inherently oppressive and in need of
complete prohibition (O'Brien 2019).

To address this issue in a realistic manner, I also want to take
some distance from the discourses of abolition or segregation,
which either aim to abolish the family as a key component of society or detach themselves from the dominant social fabric and
economic regime. Far from falling into the charming poetics of

insurrection, the approach I will develop here is an integrated and transitional one. In this era in which politics is more and more driven by emotions and affects, it may be counterproductive to base a strategy of social change on the rational claim of defining better social and economic institutions: transformation must happen in the realm of the cosmopolitical, in our psychosocial patterns of relation. In that sense, locating, orienting, and stimulating gradual, qualitative changes might be more productive than succumbing to the dangerously appealing siren song of the revolution.

Therefore, a consequent, informed critique must look at the sociomaterial conditions in which we currently operate in order to later articulate a transitional alternative model. Following Kathi Weeks (Red May TV 2020), this is what I propose to develop by looking at the three components that constitute the current hegemonic regime of social reproduction, or what she calls the family paradigm:

1. Family as a privatized system of household-based social reproduction;
2. The couple form;
3. The privileging of biogenetic-centered kinship.

Firstly, I will look at the implications of the family household as the private socio-economic normative unit of society. This point has already been touched upon briefly, and it's clear that a study of the ways in which architectural and urban politics historically sustained that specific order would reach beyond the scope of this book. Nonetheless, a quick articulation of the inherent violence of this organizing principle, as well as a brief review of recent alternative developments, will inform the next chapter.

Secondly, I propose a fundamental critique of the desirability of the couple-form to organize the reproduction of life and look at different frameworks that challenge mononormativity by seeing how non-monogamous practices can unlock mechanisms of care — a rebuilding of empathy and sensitivity whose benefits reach beyond human social formations and provide leads in solving issues related to our relation to non-human ecologies.

Thirdly, I look at the norm of biogenetic kinship and see how this naturalized field of desire remains largely culturally unchallenged, even though some of its aspects are being shaken by feminist critique as well as recent medical technocapitalist developments.

1. social Reproduction and the Household

The private family household is nowadays the main place of violence and abuse in contemporary western society, with important correlation between intimate partner violence and child abuse (Gracia et al. 2020). This is the direct result of our patriarcho-capitalist culture as well as an important matter for feminist politicians and activists, since researchers have shown that there exists a direct and significant correlation between a country's level of gender equality and rates of domestic violence (Esquivel-Santoveña, Lambert, and Hamel 2013). To inform our reflection on this topic, let's first look at what happens when this phenomenon is temporarily intensified by external conditions — for example, a pandemic that forces many to stay at home.

The confined family

The Covid-19 outbreak of 2020 is a perfect illustration of the social issues at stake with the culture of the nuclear, private family. As confinement measures were largely deployed in attempts to contain the pandemic, authorities observed a massive surge of domestic violence around the world (Campbell 2020). In some cases in France and Italy, hotels were requisitioned as shelters for those fleeing abuse from their households (Usher et al. 2020, 549). But, as a rule, people had to follow the imperative of "stay at home," a concept whose homogeneity of material implications can maybe apply to those who made up these policies but definitely not to all. In that context, the family has been the stage for a generalized retreat that only consolidated the dynamics I previously described as the privatization of care, a tendency in which the family household is increasingly mobilized as a safety net for the ravaging socio-economic impacts of neoliberal politics.

Confinement produces the feeling of a diminished perceptive world in which horizons are physically and metaphorically reduced to spatiotemporal immediateness, in stark contrast to the baffling, global media circus leading individuals to the feeling of a complete lack of agency. What this reinforces is a concentration of attention focused on family members, exacerbated by this withdrawal from the productive friction of both the public space and the democratic agora. In the context of reduced social interactions, proximity with the household members can concentrate social expectations and frustrations toward a few, as well as practices of empathy, listening, and awareness. These caring and less caring practices are often framed in the hierarchical context of patriarchal filiation.

The risk then is that the power relations inherent to the hierarchical structure of the family lead to situations in which parents are driven into letting their stress and tensions be discharged onto their children. Think about it: there is no other scenario in which "grown-up," supposedly reasonable people let themselves act as absolute authoritative figures to another human being — with the exception, of course, of other cases of infantilization by institutionalized figures of authority, which themselves are most often modeled on the figure of the authoritative father: the teacher, the judge, the doctor. Note that in its common meaning, the word itself, infantilization, clearly signifies the act of subordinating another person in a hierarchical power relation. In a different (and possible!) culture, in which these metaphysics of domination would not apply, it may have for example meant to rejuvenate. Concepts are never neutral.

De-privatize the Family

The challenge, then, is to shift from a culture of domination to a culture of connection, to develop horizontality in our relations. In the context of confinement and social distancing measures, it might be the right time to think about the implications of such a program, that is, to de-privatize the family in order to protect its weakest members from the isolation and invisibilization produced by the opacity of its enclosed form.

Of course, there is one obvious field of inquiry that must be addressed: architecture. Indeed, it is a hard realization that heteronormativity is basically what shaped the evolution of our western urban landscapes over the last centuries, by inscribing prevailing notions of respectable domesticity and family into the materiality of our cities (Oswin 2010). Queering architecture will be one of the major challenges in stepping out of this status quo. This topic would exceed the frame of this book, but current developments in cooperative housing are pointing at a future when collectivizing housing and care might be a fruitful approach, notably with regard to the challenges raised by our increasing and aging population. Many researchers are currently investigating this issue (Hester and Srnicek 2017; Schwarz and Sabatier-Schwarz 2017; Hede 2017).

Lexically speaking, it might be a good idea to get rid of the abstraction of "public" vs. "private" sphere, as it really did not do us any justice so far. Might the terms "intimate" vs. "societal" be more appropriate to describe the distinction between two realms of codified socialization? In both cases, one must be accountable for oneself; no shadiness allowed. Or, should we get rid of any strict boundary between the two? What analytical tools do we need, and which words should we use? For that matter, there is another very simple discursive habit that I think we should get rid of as soon as possible: the possessiveness implied by the obnoxious phrasing "having a child" (or "*getting* a child" in Dutch and German). This linguistic privatization and objectification of the child as something that is owned and thus subordinated — a real oppression hidden behind the phraseology of cuteness, historically linking children with women in their shared subordination — is the most obvious illustration of the violence inscribed in our culture of generationality, in which one generation is "possessed" by another.

The myth of childhood

An important feminist work that challenged the foundations of the conventional heterosexual nuclear family is Shulamith Firestone's landmark book *The Dialectic of Sex* (1970). Her radical intervention, aligned with the revolutionary affects of that time and rightly outdated for today's standards in terms of old-school freudism, essentialism, and heterocentrism, still conveys a relevant discourse for our reflection around childhood. Indeed, she saw the myth of childhood as reinforced by the result of compulsory education and the increasing privatization of family life. She convincingly describes school as a space in which hierarchy and competitiveness, underlining children's subordinate status in relation to adults, prepares them for their insertion into a hierarchical and inegalitarian social order. Additionally, she shows how the confinement of children within families, schools, and other specialist settings limits their horizon, with their lives being permanently supervised and circumscribed by adults.

She also saw economic dependence as central to the oppression of children, arguing that children's dependence on parental patronage is a source of humiliation. Indeed, in a society where individual autonomy is valued, dependence is a marker of less than fully human status (at that time, this "fully human" status was still in most cases the privilege of the white, male adult). Importantly, since the 1970s, the economic dependence as well as surveillance and regulation of children has, if anything, intensified. Compulsory schooling has been prolonged further since Firestone's era and current economic conditions make it more difficult for even more privileged young people to live without parental support (Jackson 2010, 120), and anxiety about children's safety and development seems to be at an all-time high.

Childhood, then, is not simply a natural state of immaturity or an age category but a social status defined by social and economic dependence, subjection to adult authority, and exclusion from adult citizenship rights. Childhood in our culture can best be described as the production phase of adult capitalist subjects: "growing up" under capitalism is basically a process of unlearning empathy, of preparing oneself for taking part in a social order of exploitation and competition. Firestone's bold attack against childhood, pertinent in the context of her time, might show some weaknesses in regard to its radicality. Nonetheless, it helps us to question the romanticization of childhood and to think about why childhood is the only form of social subordination valorized as a state of freedom (Jackson 2010, 122).

Generational Isolation

So, this age-segregated organization of society results from a culture that naturalizes childhood, one in which elders feel legitimate in being useless on the basis of their place in the generational hierarchy and by the principle of meritocracy. People would rather suffer and wait until they are retired to enjoy an idle state of life — "I worked all my life for this" — than to rebel and change the labor conditions that make their life miserable for a large section of what we call "adulthood."

We have seen earlier how the western patriarchal culture produces intense social isolation at the dusk of a normative lifetime. Again, this is largely caused by this social institution we call "family." As a household-based social reproduction order that displaces individuals based on their position in the hierarchy of generations, it means that when time is due, there is little agency to be found in terms of negotiating living conditions for the aging subject. The elderly home model, which raises questions on a fundamental level in terms of quality of life, reveals the complete failure of our society to develop decency in our inter-generational relational practices.

In order to foster a less hierarchical society, we may have first to look at the implications in the psychosocial development of children produced by the age segregation that rhythmizes their lives during more than a decade of mandatory schooling, through which they are constrained in constant and unilateral relationships of subordination with adults. Equally important as the many initiatives of experimental schooling that distribute agency to every person involved, it seems urgent to reconsider this absolute segregation by age and develop more opportunities of inter-generational complicity and collaboration, established in de-hierarchicalized and non-patriarchal ways.

> *Perhaps one always experienced the parental generation as harmless and disempowered, once the latter's physical energy subsided, while one's own generation seemed to be threatened by youth: in the antagonistic society, the relationship of the generations is also one of competition, behind which stands naked violence.*
>
> — Adorno (1974, 1–2)

2. The couple-form and the capitalist scheme of Love

> *The couple-form has historically been valorized and conventionalized, so that it is the very essence of 'normal.' Whether a person is coupled or not is fundamental to their experience of social recognition and belonging: the good citizen is the coupled citizen, and the socially integrated, psychologically developed and well-functioning person is coupled. Being part of a couple is widely seen and felt to be an achievement, a stabilizing status characteristic of adulthood, indicative of moral responsibility and bestowing full membership of the community. To be outside the couple-form is, in many ways, to be outside, or at least on the margins of, society.*
>
> — Roseneil et al. (2020, 4)

> *[I]n the modern United States, and the places its media forms influence, to different degrees, the fantasy world of romance*

> *is used normatively — as a rule that legislates the boundary*
> *between a legitimate and valuable mode of living/loving and all*
> *the others. The reduction of life's legitimate possibility to one plot*
> *is the source of romantic love's terrorizing, coercive, shaming,*
> *manipulative, or just diminishing effects — on the imagination as*
> *well as on practice.*
>
> — Berlant (2012, 87)

The dyadic couple remains one of the most potent objects of normativity in contemporary western societies. The cultural norm of exclusive romantic love, that expanded in the course of modernity, produces an artificial scarcity of affection that supports the considerable market built around it, from the wedding industry — the best day (to spend money) of your life! — to the most contemporary manifestation of this phenomenon, where this artificial scarcity is algorithmically optimized by online dating apps in order to keep individuals in this perpetual state of dissatisfaction (David and Cambre 2016). Fundamentally, these companies have to design products that encourage a culture of volatile relationality, otherwise they would simply run out of business. This is a perfect construction built around the romantic paradigm as based on a fantasy that both engenders the lack (the absence of what is promised in the fantasy) and the desire (to find something that will supply the lack). Furthermore, our societal frustration and obsession with sex is capitalized upon by advertising agencies and entertainment companies further fueling consumerist logics.

In this context, love finds itself being increasingly engineered by a few programmers in the silly valley, a highly dubious ideological space mostly populated with people (white, rich, men) who might not be the most critically and politically aware. Dating apps are also relevant in revealing the embedding of a capitalist conditioning in our relational practices, especially today as online dating is becoming the most popular way for couples to meet (Rosenfeld, Thomas, and Hausen 2019, 17753). The semantics deployed are eloquent and reveal the confluence of an economic and predatory mindset in the way the "business" of dating and mating is articulated: a field populated by scores, values, quantities; by the terms "investment," "marketability," "supply"; and by the values of speed and accumulation.

Conceptually, this universe reveals itself as a sort of celebration of the neoliberal figure of the "entrepreneur," which associates subjective agency with sexual power. Moreover, each relationship appears as a short-term investment, which like any investment can be good or bad, profitable or loss-making. More precisely, we have a mode of interaction anchored in the immediate demand for affective profit, for a surplus of enjoyment (de Castro 2014), in which (self-)objectification and reification are banalized. This paradigm is maybe best exemplified by the French dating site *Adopte un Mec* ("Adopt a Guy," http://www.adopteunmec.com/), whose marketing strategy, while capitalizing on a feminist rhetoric of women's empowerment, epitomizes this paradigm of uninhibited objectification by deploying the concept of a virtual supermarket, with a "shopping cart" to be filled with "products." The calls are all in line with a purely commercial enterprise: "Boutique ouverte 24/7" ("Shop open 24/7"), "Livraison rapide" ("Fast delivery"), "Mise en panier illimitée" ("shopping without limits"), "Des nouveautés tous les jours" ("Novelties every day").

Nonetheless, the ideal of the couple prevails, as dyadic monogamy still represents the privileged and hegemonic relational form enshrined in our culture and laws. Again, it appears logical that our economic system based on artificial scarcity is to be supported by a regime of desire based on simulated or engineered lack. In the heteronormative society, sex is presented both as an omnipresent call and a rare commodity, which, when it can only take place within the couple, makes the latter the object of the greatest covetousness and anxiety as to its attainment and perpetuation. Thus the couple is presented to us as the holy grail, something that must be chased and preserved, as the mob of ideological therapists who work to maintain it at all costs enjoin us to do (Stayton 1985).

Even though evolutions in gender identification and romantic relationship models are shaking the stability of the heterosexual dyad as the undisputed mode of romance, they often produce identities and relations considerably patterned on their heteronormative counterparts. This is the result of a society in which the codes of heterosexuality and patriarchy are embodied and omnipresent. Psychological development in this culture results in a strong grip of heteronormativity over most individuals, which itself sustains insensitivities fueling a capitalist relational mindset. The romantic love model produces relationships in the manner of great seabirds producing guano. It is the fertilizer of a capitalist vision of intimacy escalated into the norm of the private nuclear family.

Through their fieldwork with children, researchers Carol Gilligan and Naomi Snider (2018) have shown that the initiation into the gendered roles of patriarchy subverts the ability to repair relational ruptures by enjoining men to separate their minds from their emotions (thus not to think what they are feeling) and women to remain silent (thus not to say what they know). Rather than universalizing Gilligan's analysis, which would naturalize western subjectivities and consolidate a binary epistemology of gender, I propose to make use of her empirical work to make claims regarding the current heteronormative model of patriarchy and its possible contestation.

Non-monogamy: A Political Act

Monogamy is the ground on which the whole culture of patriarchal heteronormativity is built. Religion, sexology, psychology, law, and popular science all play a part in the naturalization of monogamy as the only normal, healthy, and moral way to maintain a romantic relationship (Rothschild 2018). As a quick reminder, this is a purely cultural construct as Murdock (1949) famously reported that only forty-three of 238 human societies have monogamy as their ideal. If monogamy persists in our society, it is because of its ideological function, raising romantic love as the only possible prospect of wellbeing. In that sense, challenging compulsory monogamy also defies the ideology of the "happy monogamous family."

Throughout recent history, the status quo has been increasingly challenged by western sexual subcultures. In academic circles, the emergence of research around the concept of consensual non-monogamy (CNM) has revealed the extent of this cultural phenomenon, even if these counter-hegemonic practices are mostly deployed by white, educated, and middle-class people (Rubin et al. 2014). Additionally, these practices are not immune to assimilation in normative, capitalist culture. Although they increase the visibility of sexual subcultures within the public domain, popular relationship self-help texts often reinforce a "monogamous-style" of relating that emphasizes the primacy of heterosexual dyadic commitment within CNM relationships (Wilkinson 2010).

Nonetheless, the refusal of monogamy is increasingly performed as a political gesture in defiance of heteronormative practices of belonging and of assimilationist tendencies which absorb the diversity of queer sexual and affective relations into the hegemonic model of the couple and nuclear family. Of course, this refusal is often permitted by a privileged position in terms of social validation, in opposition to the vulnerable state that pushes queer people into socially approved monogamy in the first place. In this latter case, compliance with the normative scheme of life provides queers with social recognition and approbation, instead of rejection and devalorization.

The democratization of non-monogamous lifestyles might reduce the tendencies I just mentioned. On the other hand, it may also produce new types of normative hierarchies and patterns of exclusion, as can already be observed within some (relatively marginal) social circles in which monogamy is dismissed as conservative or outdated. I'm not here to make any judgment, and I don't think that any personal choice in terms of relationship style should be a valid reason for social exclusion. However, I believe that there is definitely some potential in non-monogamous practices to collectively challenge sedimented patterns of toxic relationality. In the semantics of recent alternatives to monogamy, two models seem to have emerged: polyamory and relationship anarchy. Let's unwrap what these two frameworks may provide as tools for emancipating from our patriarcho-capitalist relational habits.

polyamory

Polyamory emerged as a concept in the 1990s with the growth of a community committed to a form of non-monogamy in which multiple emotional and sexual attachments are supported and valued. Polyamory as a theoretical framework consists of a set of guidelines for an ethical form of non-monogamy that requires consent, honesty, commitment, boundary-setting, and agreement negotiation (Hammack, Frost, and Hughes 2019). In that sense, the term polyamory has opened a stable cultural space to cultivate a legitimate alternative to the norm of the couple-form, with its complex lexicon, growing literature, media visibility, and global community.

Elizabeth Larsen (1998) describes polyamory in these terms: "an outgrowth of both the group marriage and communal living movements of the 1960s and '70s, the still-young polyamory movement espouses the value of committed, loving relationships with more than one partner." Larsen also shares that increasing numbers of young adults are trying out polyamory as an alternative to their parents' failed monogamous relations. Indeed, polyamory can be seen as a movement in opposition to both the traditional, romantic couple model, and to the "swinger" communities that emerged in the 1960s and '70s, more generally straight and focused on sexuality. Additionally, Jade Aguilar's (2013) ethnography of two communal groups of poly practitioners revealed the way in which group members engaged in "ideological work" associated with feminism and the repudiation of traditional institutions like marriage.

We can observe some similarity between the emerging polyamorous subject and the modern lesbian one, in the sense that they both got confronted with the violence of normative sociability. Talking about a series of cases depicted in the media of that times prior the intelligibility of the lesbian subject, Lisa Duggan writes that they "faced hostility and opposition not only from pathologizing sexologists and patriarchal social institutions but also from their closest female relatives and friends. In addition, they all struggled to establish a reciprocal love relationship with another woman who did not fully share their commitment to a life outside the traditional heterosexual family" (1993, 808). This resonates with the multiple accounts I received of polyamorous people whose romantic affections were directed toward some-one whose emancipation from mononormative cultural codes was not consolidated yet, with the anxiety-inducing tension ly-ing in the possibility of that person turning back to the norma-tive comfort of the couple-form.

Additionally, even many who practice consensual non-monogamy appear to privilege monogamy as an ideal, likely internalizing stigma about their own non-normative practices. As polyamory often reproduces the structure of the couple, it presents limits in terms of emancipation. As such, it is a cul-ture that, to a certain extent, maintains the myth of romantic love and thus constitutes a watered-down form of more radical approaches to deconstructing that norm. Nevertheless, my en-counters with researchers and practitioners of polyamory have allowed me to identify certain aspects of this practice that allow us to free ourselves from patriarchal relational logics.

In its emphasis on radical transparency and communication, polyamory can give space to a mode of communication that transcends the limits of patriarchal psychological mechanisms, as it pushes men to be connected to their emotions, and women to express theirs. Following the thesis that Gilligan and Snider (2018) famously developed — wherein men are disconnected from their emotions while women's true voices are silenced, a thesis supported by an accumulation of research suggesting that women continue to do the bulk of emotional work in het-erosexual relationships (Duncombe and Marsden 1993; Horne and Johnson 2019) — the polyamorous framework of relation might provide a valuable set of tools and steps to overcome the kind of insensitive relational patterns of our patriarchal culture.

For example, this immediately relates to the matter of consent, through a scheme that is really heteronormativity 101: women who don't know how to say "no" without feeling anxiety or guilt and men unable to hear a "no" or to receive it positively.

From my own experience, I can say that polyamory has represented a consequential asset in my journey of deconstructing my masculinity. Indeed, for a polyamorous relationship to function in a healthy and satisfying way, it is inescapable to allow oneself to feel vulnerable. This may sound funny, but it is not an easy thing to do for men conditioned to maintain a facade of unbreakable and unreachable strength in their social life. Furthermore, you have to be able to listen to your own body, as well as receiving and processing spoken and unspoken signals from your partners. These types of somatic and emotional intelligence are skills that have to be learned, and polyamorous relationships can provide a caring environment to facilitate that process. Honestly, I would be curious to experience life under a political regime in which people who govern us would be polyamorous; it seems to me that the desensitized, pseudo-rational disembodied form of subjectivity that is dominant in the high spheres of politics would benefit from such a practical apprenticeship of sensitivity, attention, and self-awareness.

From a feminist perspective, polyamory can be the stage of an emancipatory narrative, in which women trapped in heterosexual monogamous relationships with abusive or "toxic" masculine partners are given a potential, culturally legible way out. Indeed, this is one of the syndromes of a culture that privileges long monogamous relationships, where the lack of space for experimentation maintains the status quo, that is, heterosexual relationships built on the fear of loneliness, which sustain gender inequality and violence. In this context, polyamory can act as a trigger or wake-up call toward more feminist empowerment in heterosexual relations, or even lead to lesbianism for the luckiest ones (congrats!). Actually, this is a recurring trope of polyamory: the man, driven by his libido, wants to open the relationship and ends up crying that his girlfriend left him after discovering how better the world is outside. Nevertheless, considering the existing power relations in heterosexual relationships, I would guess that polyamory still produces more pain and emotional labor for women than men, and the argument that polyamory liberates women is often voiced by sexist men in order to subjugate women to their desires. Therefore, straight women should approach polyamory with caution.

There is one important source of suffering, in terms of an emotion supported by the culture of romantic love, that polyamory challenges: jealousy. Historically speaking, jealousy as a naturalized instinct is a patriarchal construct, due to the fear of falsification of descendants (Russell 1970, 23). Men had to make sure that the children their wives were carrying were truly their own. As a result of this paranoid culture, conforming to the acknowledgment of sexual jealousy as a just and legitimate feeling promotes the most terrible authoritarian drives in the psyche of the normative lover (Cohn 2010, 415). It is an especially perverted cultural trickery to "teach" children to control their jealousy (for example, between siblings), an educational move performed in pure condescendence, only to allow ourselves the most extreme affective outbreaks as adults. This requires the institutions of romantic love and compulsory monogamy, both supported by a mythology deeply inscribed in our culture. In other words, the industry of romantic tragedy is coding our desires (and capitalizing on this process). Immersion in a different culture of sexuality can be one way to make the social constructedness of such a "natural" feeling as sexual jealousy vividly clear (for example, Wekker 1999, 128). Thanks to its growing accessibility and legibility, polyamory provides such a frame for the occidental subject.

When sacralized as a legitimate feeling, sexual jealousy propels logics of possessiveness and competitiveness in our relational practices. It infuses a predatorial regime of control and opacity into our relationships. To deconstruct the feeling of jealousy through the open communication and self-attention that comes with the untangling of a polyamorous existence can be tremendously productive in terms of alignment with our feelings. It is also a good schoolyard for wannabe democratic subjects, since it provides the stage for the miniaturized rehearsal of an agonistic society (Mouffe 1999), one in which conflicting interests are necessarily taken into consideration for the wellbeing of all. Nonetheless, it is a hell of a task to tackle the deep cultural conditioning we have been submitted to by the ideology of romance, and polyamory can provoke harsh love-related traumas if not handled carefully. For that reason mainly, polyamory should not be seen as a universal breakthrough that everyone should pursue, considering the indoctrination that most of us have deeply internalized regarding the exclusivity of romance, intimacy, and sexuality. There is no easy way.

Three last things must be said about polyamory. First, when compared to the framework of romantic love that relies on the dyadic association of the couple wherein two people blend into a single unit for society, polyamorous practitioners are often criticized and perceived as guilty of disenchanting love for the sake of favoring a more individualistic posture. While romance in the past functioned as a cultural tool to reinforce the division of labor, polyamory can be conceived as a reaction to the flexibility required by our neoliberal era, characterized by an increasing necessity of mobility and rapid adaptation to changing conditions of labor — in austerity times, better not put all one's eggs into one basket. Thus, while polyamory as a psychosocial practice has potential to break down barriers to solidarity, it might on the opposite side reinforce a sort of radical individualism, inscribed in the neoliberal atomization of the social. There lies its ambivalent status regarding capitalism: while it partly feeds into its ideological expansion of instrumental relationships, disrupting the little social responsibility left outside of market relations — at least that's the argument deployed by some of its communist critiques — it also challenges romantic exclusivity as one of the most wide-spread expressions of propertarianism.

Secondly, polyamory can also be a privileged site for toxic dynamics of narcissistic and manipulative behaviors. At worst, it can feed a megalomaniacal logic of partner accumulation, or be palliatively summoned by the desperate fear of intimate scarcity that is prevalent in the loneliness of our times. As a framework of intimacy inherently subjected to chronic as well as persistent imbalances, especially in the case of heterosexual relations, it raises considerable risks of establishing power relations with painful consequences. As Brigitte Vasallo (2017), a vocal researcher and activist in defense of non-monogamy warns us: "If being polyamorous is just having several relationships [...] without deep reflection on how we relate, the same patterns will be reproduced and worse, will be multiplied, with all their forms of oppression and abuse."

Thirdly, it is important to raise the demographic specificity of polyamory. In that regard, research indicates the significance of class and race privilege, as poly communities are found to be predominantly white, highly educated, and middle class (Klesse 2014, 208). This can mainly be explained by the fact that stepping out from the conventions of compulsory monogamy requires a certain degree of economic and cultural self-assurance mostly provided by a privileged social environment. Generally, racialized and working-class people are more likely to be exposed to stigmatization if they publicly assume non-monogamous identities. It is also the case that polyamory is more easily pursued by men than women, considering the still culturally prevalent gender bias that associates women's free sexuality with frivolity and men's with power.

To conclude, polyamory can support a progressive agenda by providing a reclamation of emotional sensitivity and communicational capacity from the wounds of a patriarchal education and socialization. As a relational framework, it can model sexual or romantic relationships devoid of some of the patriarchal features of mononormative culture. Nonetheless, its practice is not immune to severe cases of abuse and is accessible to only a reduced part of the population. Furthermore, the sanctity of sex and the evaluation of romantic relationships above all others is mostly left unchallenged. This is precisely what our next turn of inquiry promises to address.

Relationship Anarchy

Since we are dealing with the matter of composing a relational ethic nourished by a mentality that seeks to free reality from all relations of institutionalized domination, it is opportune to orient ourselves toward the anarchist tradition. Following that same agenda, theorists of anarchism have long been emphasizing the fact that anarchism should not only develop alternatives to capitalism and the state, but must also offer a "radical reorganization of sexuality," one that does not chain people down with supposedly stable identities as a result of their sexual or gender practices, then create hierarchies of value out of those identities (Shannon and Willis 2010, 434). Nothing in society will be changed if the mechanisms of power that function outside, below, and alongside the state apparatuses, on a much more minute and everyday level, are not also changed (Foucault 1980, 60).

This is where the anarchist meets the queer, in their shared appeal to the political possibilities of pleasure. Both anarchism and queer theory borrow from a range of influences to support a politics of freedom (Shepard 2010, 515) and argue for a need to move beyond hierarchical and naturalized arrangements of socially constructed identities. While we could look into the many axes through which anarchist thinkers have approached this matter, including ones often overlooked such as asexuality (Fahs 2010) or friendship (Evans 2016), I want to focus on the emerging concept that supplements the framework offered by polyamory to develop more ethical intimacies, namely "relationship anarchy." What it promises us is an emancipatory path from the hegemonic stylization of desire operated by heteronormative love. As Preciado (2018) writes: "Enjoy your aesthetics of domination, but don't try to turn your style into a law." Especially with an anarchist.

Relationship (or relational) anarchy (RA), as one of the practical and theoretical frameworks that have been developed within the field of consensual non-monogamy, consists in a rejection of the paradigm of romance that is still prevalent among the ranks of most polyamorous practitioners. This implies a refusal of three types of hierarchies (de las Heras Gómez 2019, 2): romance supremacism (giving a higher status to intimate relationships with romantic elements), sexual supremacism (giving a higher status to intimate relationships with sexual elements), and hierarchically ranking romantic-sexual relationships (as in the idea of "primary" versus "secondary" partners often observed in polyamorous constellations, especially in those emerging from a heteronormative background).

Insofar as RA consists in a rejection of the categories that compartmentalize emotional bonds between relationship models such as "couple," "lovers," or "friends," it also challenges the distribution of symbolic value (status, prestige) assigned to each bond according to its coding in the patriarchal heteronormative order. It refuses the idea of a romantic exclusive relationship as a universally shared goal. Politically, this refusal of the couple privilege (Garhan 2013) raises the issue of questioning the body of social, legal, and financial advantages accorded to that specific normative arrangement. It also sheds light on the concentration of resources (economic, care, emotional, time) that is inherent to it.

The radicality in RA is that its political philosophy is to denaturalize love conceived as an ideological construct in order to unravel the type of social organization (symbolic, material, legal) that it sustains (de las Heras Gómez 2019). The most dangerous aspect of the romantic love ideology is that it shapes a vision of love as an exclusive, quantitative asset. By refusing this conception and reclaiming love as the primary affective register in social interaction, RA opens a space to reconsider the social distribution of resources, through a redistribution of affection. In its ideal form, RA is the project of universal respect. In that relationship anarchists advocate for a radically inclusive and modular regime of attention and empathy, RA seems to open the way to an extended regime of sensitivity.

Indeed, this strategic refusal of (any or specific) transcendental social roles — girlfriend and boyfriend, husband and wife, but also mother and father or parent and children — serves as a call for criticality and invention in the design of our affective formations. It emphasizes situated, individual, and collective agency in departing from expected social behavior regarding family members, lovers, friends, neighbors, colleagues, or classmates, up to clerks and passersby. For example, the Free Hugs movement could be understood as a form of RA. In terms of education, RA thus constitutes an excellent framework to start thinking the socialization of kids outside of the nuclear family style of support and care.

Of course, RA is difficult to implement in real life because of both normative social pressure and internal conditioning. In a capitalist society, fostering a social regime where status-oriented, possessive, and instrumental relationships are the norm, relationship anarchists run the risk of being caught up in these toxic dynamics whenever they attempt to make connections outside of their RA circles. This makes them particularly vulnerable to disillusionment and violence or imposes upon them a radical distanciation from non-RA practitioners, even though they themselves can never be fully emancipated from these patriarcho-capitalist relational logics. Much like polyamory, RA is a relentless process of (un)learning and reflexivity. As an anarchist praxis, RA serves as a joyful emancipatory reaction to the capitalization of sociability that occurs through neoliberal subjectivation. It serves as a conceptual tool to operate the internal denaturalization of romantic love, to which I will return below.

(Re-)eroticize the world

Even if they offer us glimpses of more universal sentiments, polyamory and RA are still very much focused on improving the benevolence of our relational practices in the realm of human interactions. To add to this, I embrace this imperative formulation — re-eroticize the world! — in order to restore unchained desire above consumerist and egoistic enjoyment. What it means is to performatively enact the affective investment of being as part of the world, in opposition to the idea of being "in" the world, as if we were singular entities arranged in a Euclidean and linear spacetime. For this I honestly haven't found any more direct tool than drugs and especially LSD, but of course there are other ways. Living in exhilarating symbiosis with the world fully challenges the metaphysics of individualism; to re-eroticize the world is to start to embrace this ontological connection. To be clear, I am not talking about hippies hugging trees, even though that is also nice, but denaturalizing romantic love through the exercise of alternative modes of affection is probably a more potent political praxis.

Once again, I will make a point by advocating for an intervention in the realm of language. Most of my readers have probably heard about the phenomenon of gender-neutral pronouns and their increasing usage by cis people to support their non-binary peers. What this has opened is a window of language creativity in a category of words generally considered as a "closed class" — a group of words whose number rarely grows and whose meanings rarely change (Blaylock 2020). Seduced by this phenomenon and the rise of neopronouns, I started to ponder how this might represent an opportunity for shifting away from problematic habits of thought.

In English, there is a hard linguistic distinction between humans or subjects (he, she, they) and non-humans or objects (it), where the pronoun for "it" is considered a slur when used to designate a subject. This thus performatively reinforces the internalized hierarchy between humans and non-humans, as well as the metaphysics of property (objects subordinated to subjects) that historically went through a colonial and patriarchal process of universalization. This linguistic status quo is an obvious mark of disrespect for our non-human kins and might be a sort of cognitive bulwark against any radical shift away from the ingrained western mentality that prioritizes culture over nature. Inscribed in the imperial language of global capital, human exceptionalism today serves the agenda of extractive capitalism.

I started to think of a semantic gesture that would aim at countering the harmful metaphysics of the subject. Relatedly, I heard some vegans call animals "people" in a linguistic move against human exceptionalism. Going one step further, as a radical materialist, I refuse any form of metaphysical hierarchy between different matter(s). Therefore, why not use the pronoun "it" to mark my belonging to the world and refuse our linguistic hierarchy that puts humans on a pedestal? What if this new social ritual of affirming personal pronouns could be seized as an opportunity to open a space for dialogue around this topic? I already jump for joy at the idea of sharing the same pronoun with plants, minerals, and non-human biological entities. We could call everything, everyone "it." No hierarchy. Let's plunge into the matter: *it!*

That is when I realized that trans politics are unfortunately entangled with my philosophical concerns. Indeed, calling someone "it" is culturally perceived as a mark of dehumanization. Historically, this resonates with the colonial identification of Black people as property. In today's society, it is at the heart of the trauma many trans people have experienced in being subjected to a transphobic culture that often defines them as "less than human." There are two reasons why my embrace of "it" is problematic: first, that it might trigger or generate pain; second, as someone who is seen as white and regularly as cis, it is highly questionable whether I am legitimate in reclaiming the term. By appropriating an avenue painstakingly built by gender activists to lightly serve my own agenda, I might be taking the risk of going against their own politics. A last additional issue comes from the BDSM community, where the usage of the "it" pronoun is often consensually negotiated as part of objectification and dehumanization experiences. Therefore, one might feel uncomfortable calling me "it" in daily public encounters if that, for them, is the signifying marker of a private or sexual practice.

So, sadly, the world is not ready for the "it" revolution. I do not have any prescriptive statement to make about pronouns. We need to develop other strategies to tackle the pernicious linguistic distinction between people and things. But I hope my little thought experiment opened reflection on this matter, as well as constituting a smooth transition into the next section of this chapter, also concerned with the supremacy of (human) biology in our culture.

3. The privileging of biogenetic-centered kinship

> *In our intensely individualistic, competitive, capitalist society,*
> *love and concern for others become inappropriate outside our*
> *very own small family groupings. Class privilege and racist*
> *exclusion are most frequently justified, by both women and men,*
> *in terms of the interests of one's own children.*
>
> — Segal (1987, 5)

I will now address the most symptomatic and insidious aspect of the patriarchal organization, namely the privilege granted in particular to those who reproduce this social order, fathers. I focus on them, but my invective also extends to other members of the heteronormative community. For this demonstration, I make use of personal observations of the specific social environments in which I operate, art and education, before delving into the symbolic order that privileges biogenetic reproduction in our culture.

The reproduction of the lame

My starting point is here: why do so many dull people nonetheless take up teaching or decision-making positions, and see themselves sought, hired, and promoted to the detriment of other individuals whose work I often find much more stimulating? How does this selection take place? Well, I realized that it was significantly, and particularly in the most insipid cases, individuals who had recently obtained the status of parent.

This unfortunate selection can thus be explained by two factors. The first is the economic imperative of having to care for a child. Suddenly, fathers are forced to push themselves into these positions in order to provide for their households and therefore work harder to obtain them. For sure, they are not the only boring people around. And of course, some of them are very worthy people. Nevertheless, this is really a strong pattern I've observed while approaching my thirties: the dullness of the successful, exhausted father. But the reason why I'm sharing this is because it is due to another factor, one that mainly explains how these young fathers achieve higher status in society, which is to me the core of patriarchy. This factor is that these positions are transmitted from older patriarchs to younger fathers, thus reproducing this order of masculine authority in a naturalized form of leadership.

Indeed, it is only by having children that these fathers can reach the last step on the heteronormative script of life, thus gaining the ultimate form of virility, which is being the successful entrepreneurs of the procreation business. This then conditions the distribution of social roles by decision-makers (usually the previous generation of fathers) based on this symbolic order that associates fatherhood with professionalism. This is the mechanism through which fathers transmit these high-status positions from one generation to the other, in addition to all the other pernicious logics of cronyism that take place in social reproduction.

So, patriarchy is bad and, in many regards, very bad. It creates oppression, inequality, violence, disconnection, impoverished relational practices, and so on. But one reason that is not often raised and should federate everyone against this fiasco is precisely that patriarchy is profoundly favoring dull and boring people, those most indoctrinated with bourgeois ideology, pushing them in the center of the stage, people you don't want to have in positions of decision-making or hyper-visibility. And it is not even their fault, since they have usually so much pressure on their shoulders. These fathers have been trained, and they are conditioned to exercise their authority in order to pursue the glory of their now old-and-afraid-to-die fathers through their own success. They are gluttonous, authority-craving addicts. They want to have kids upon which they can impose their authority, and when this happens, society throws more authority at them. The patriarch is the authority whore for whom fatherhood is the ultimate performative act, repeating a codified social pattern that reinforces authority through the citation of a prior, authoritative set of relational practices.

This is the fundamental aspect of patriarchy — transmission — which goes beyond that of domination more widely denounced by the defenders of the feminist cause. Fathers who recognize and support each other, maintaining themselves in the privileged spheres of power, and by extension those who provide for this reproductive role by conforming to the heterosexual family model. Kinship is thus a passport to dignity in patriarchal culture, a condition that exacerbates any biological factors that would push individuals to form a couple or to give birth. This is where my efforts are directed, in terms of resolving the issues related to the hegemony of this reproductive formation that reach beyond questions of gender and sexuality.

Even in a speculative, post-gender society, one in which all gender inequalities would be erased, in which the agenda of identity politics would be ultimately accomplished and everyone could be whatever sort of neoliberal subject of their choice, we can make the hypothesis that this pattern of valorizing the reproductive parents and their offspring would still persist. When deploying feminist strategies of change, we tend to focus on masculine domination, on advocating for more horizontal gender relations; however the struggle against patriarchy is more profound and touches on patterns of exclusion and hierarchy that are more closely related to class privilege and social reproduction, and thus more difficult to address in the sphere of middle-class feminist discourse. Indeed, resistance to the nuclear family model in academic, intellectual, and artistic discourse is constrained by the fact that it constitutes the common background of virtually everyone in the western cultural elite. Its continuation is the condition, and the warranty, of conserving their privileges in economic and symbolic capital. This is why critical social theory must consist of a self-reflexive exercise, aware that it emerges out of the same object that it inquires into (Poyares 2021, 359). In this context, reproductive meritocracy should be understood for what it is, that is, a culturally specific value system from which we should attempt to disidentify urgently.

The Naturalization of Filiation

Since antiquity, western cultures have attributed a substantial importance to so-called "natural" links (Fine and Martial 2010). Following the metaphysics of blood touched upon earlier, in medieval imagery, the figure of the tree represented the concept of lineage: "like a sap, the trickle of blood that flows between generations and welds them into a community" (Klapisch-Zuber 2000, 323). In this ideology of lineage, reinforced throughout western history by christian culture to the point of eclipsing any other form of kinship, women's names are excluded since they are not allowed to inherit. It is only by giving birth that women take place in the lineage, this glorifying narrative that inscribes families in history. In this regime, female sovereignty is bound up with women's capacity to give birth. They are therefore sexually and socially subordinate, and mothers alone are sovereign, with traces of this tradition still visible in our current culture of heteronormativity.

The notion of maternal love, already present in the Middle Ages and considered "natural," slowly supplanted the ideology of lineage over the nineteenth and beginning of the twentieth centuries (Badinter 2001). As western societies evolved toward a strong industrial order with a growing need for factory workforce, the distribution of labor between men's (wage) and women's (domestic) labor led to a naturalization of gendered roles in which women's biological ability to bear children increasingly and consistently became conflated with an equivalent ability to rear children (Sherif-Trask 2010, 49).

As a result, the idea of separating children from their biological mother became a cultural taboo. Valorizing blood as a metaphor for generational lineages shifted toward the relationship between mother and child. In both cases, symbolic representations of filiation are based on biogenetic procreation of the heterosexual couple. This model, on which western juridical systems have developed throughout the centuries, produces a confusion between a legal relation (filiation as a set of legal obligations and bonding between two individuals) and the relation resulting from procreation (filiation as biological parenthood), therefore naturalizing legal filiation as a relationship necessarily modeled on heterosexuality. This supports the privatization of social reproduction through enclosing children in the opaque hierarchical structure of the family, which is then charged with the obligation to produce functional citizens.

This confusion is also often instrumentalized by nationalist discourses biologizing or racializing the nation, in countries where filiation belongs both to family law and citizenship law. In the French context, Éric Fassin (2009) speaks of a logic of naturalization of nationality that has been at work for some twenty years, partly in reaction to the growing demand for parental rights by homosexual people. In this instance, the socio-cultural model of filiation is redefined by a naturalist ideology to feed the rhetorics of anti-gay politics. Concretely, Fassin describes how some conservative agencies, in order to disallow access to adoption for homosexuals, were willing to reconsider the right to adoption for individuals and limit it to heterosexual couples.

The sacralization of the genetic or biological link between parents and their offspring, summoned in this case for the defense of a heterosexual vision of democracy, is also brought up to defend the limits of the nation, this "enlarged family" that is supposedly exposed to the constant threat of invasion. It is in anti-immigration that biology is invoked in the most reactionary way. Here again, metaphors abound, where the classic "blood of the nation" competes with the delirious notion of a "national DNA." Of course, these formulations are only voiced nowadays by the most conservative corners of the political spectrum. But with the massive migration tensions that await us with the impact of climate change, the fact that the biological family is still inscribed in most of our legal systems might increasingly become a source of violence and exclusion.

challenging the biological

Many social configurations challenge this naturalized order. Most obviously, adoptive families perform a clear separation between sexuality, procreation, and filiation. Nonetheless, it is important to note the phantasmagorical place that the birth mother continues to occupy in many instances, as she is often referred to by the adoptive mothers themselves as the child's "real mother." This shows how deeply inscribed the cult of procreative reproduction in our culture is.

New biomedical technologies like artificial insemination, in-vitro fertilization, and egg donation are also shaking the ground of "natural" reproduction, forcing us in some cases for ingenious adaptations with regard to our old systems of belief. For that matter, an interesting story is the one related to the debates concerning medically assisted procreation in Israel during the 1990s. Israel has the world's highest per capita rate of in-vitro fertilization procedures, which is only one of the many manifestations of the centrality of reproduction in judaism and jewish culture. In that context, orthodox rabbis had to deal with the religious prohibitions on masturbation and adultery in front of the then new phenomenon of sperm donation (Kahn 2000). The solution they thought up might sound surprising. In order to make this new medical technique compatible with their millennium-long religious practice, the rabbis came up with the idea to rely on the use of non-jewish sperm. The sexual prohibitions then fell by themselves. Indeed, for judaism, it is through the mother that the filiation takes place. Thus, this simple twist was enough to open access to this technology for the "reproduction" of jews (106).

Finally, I would like to add a word in regard to gestational surrogacy, as it poses the most evident challenge to the notion of "natural" filiation while simultaneously revealing the glorified cultural value of genetic filiation. Indeed, what this fetishization of genetic transmission produces is an ever-growing market of techno-medical solutions to satisfy the desires of prospective parents–consumers. There are many different strands of that current, for example the possibility for lesbian couples to follow a procedure whereby one woman donates the egg while the other carries the baby.

Even more striking is the phenomenon of commercial surrogacy, the process through which a person accepts to bear a child, often produced with the genetic material of its commissioners, in exchange for payment. This is the latest capitalist response to the demand of genetic parenthood, following the logic of outsourcing, an industry churning billions of dollars in which the commodity is biogenetic progeny. This is the topic of Sophie Lewis's (2019) brilliant book, *Full Surrogacy Now: Feminism against Family*. This work positions social reproduction as labor, thus desacralizing pregnancy to examine the material implications of naturalized views of womanhood and the associated duty of gestational work.

In many regards, commercial surrogacy represents the most crude and unsentimental form of neocolonial capitalism as a phenomenon that issues from the material and ideological premises of a globalized economy, just-in-time capitalist obstetrics and its colonial–patriarchal history. It is the advanced commodity fetish that associates the child with property for its biological buyers. Nonetheless, it opens the potential of a future in which gestation is seen less as something mystical, sacred, and associated with an essentialized womanhood. Paradoxically, it also creates a space in which our cultural obsession for genetic reproduction might be confronted in rare clarity.

De-romanticizing babies and motherhood will still be an important feminist struggle for the coming decades. The cold-blooded commodification of babies challenges our perception of what might be right and could lead to larger questions of the commodification of everything else. Simultaneously, we have to speculate about what baby-making beyond blood, private coupledom, and the gene fetish might one day look like, once the ideological spectacle of the conventional nuclear family becomes obsolete.

In any case, sacralizing biogenetic reproduction is based on very illusory scientific views, where "genealogy" is indeed a misleading discursive framing for the family. People invested in the idea of making copies of themselves might be disappointed from the news brought up by feminist biologists. Genetic replication is not really what's happening when you make babies. Actually, DNA gets scrambled more than passed on, and we are much more epigenetically shaped than what is commonly thought. In fact, *"literal reproduction is a contradiction in terms"* (Haraway 1989, 352). We might better speak of co-production. New developments in scientific research popularize a more realistic idea that what we commonly understood as a determined and stable human body is actually more of a contingent, fluid, and porous system.

Today, the multiple instances of public debate that touch on the notion of a naturalized and sacralized bio-genetic kinship are open fields of conflicting agencies, where underlying intentions are not always easy to discern, and progressive voices sometimes defend conservative ideas that conflict with a feminist or anti-capitalist agenda. Facing discourses that mobilize biocentric rhetorics to justify inegalitarian politics, an ethical vision of family would have to support the cultural shift that dissociates procreation from filiation, which would open a new era in which sexual difference and the hierarchical rhythm of generations would no longer constitute the foundation of a family.

4. conclusion

The family, as a mostly unquestioned institution in our relational landscape, poses a serious obstacle to new societal organization. Indeed, it is time for humanity to embrace the reality that most of our cultural precepts were historically shaped and we are free to rewrite them. There is joy in the fact that this cultural paradigm shift can currently be observed or glimpsed in many organizational and institutional aspects of our societies, from alternative currencies and debates around defunding the police, to gender identity and polyamory. Nonetheless, all these developments are entangled in ambiguous relations to capital and should not be conceptualized only as dynamics of resistance.

In front of the still dominant bourgeois family model and heterosexuality as political regime (Wittig 1980), it is necessary to continue to explore and articulate alternative politics of desire. There can be much enthusiasm behind the idea to disentangle the vivifying forces of joy and love from the cold apparatuses of patriarchy, compulsory heterosexuality, and capitalism. For this, we need to advocate for new types of family (Cohn 2010). To do so, I mobilize three concepts that shape a proposition that addresses this problematic relationship between social reproduction and the reproduction of capital: *queer, communal, kinship.*

III

QUEER COMMUNAL KINSHIP

*[P]refiguration offers the possibility of another experience of time,
space, interpersonal relations. [...] The medium, the movement
itself as a new medium, is the message. As prophets without
enchantment, contemporary movements practice in the present
the change they are struggling for: they redefine the meaning of
social action for the whole society.*

— Melucci (1985, 801)

*The bare fact that no steam engine was ever made entirely
by another, or two others, of its own kind, is not sufficient to
warrant us in saying that steam engines have no reproductive
system.*

— Deleuze and Guattari (1972, 343)

Queers often lack family. As they contingently pop up from normative environments, they necessarily experience mismatch in their family and ideological distance from their biological kins. Of course, a deterministic vision that individualizes queerness is to be taken with a grain of salt, and I only deploy this narrative to draw a point otherwise demonstrated by empirical data: that queer people are suffering from their immersion in heteronormative settings and that they, more often than not, are willing to change that by expanding the understanding of reproduction, filiation, household dynamics, and kinship. Add the communal component to the party and you arrive at the composition of my post-patriarchy and post-capitalist utopia — a safe space in which sensitivity and inclusivity can be rebuilt and flourish.

As a conceptual, speculative field of existence, the *queer communal kinship* formation is post-gender, post-sex, and post-race. This social structure is much more enriching, fun, and safe than the shrinking family model of lame bourgeois modernity. We will see how this speculative model specifically addresses the notion of the future. It is to be approached with an enthusiastic tone — change is happening, and the decline of the old models is irrevocable. Breaking boundaries and hierarchies, an emergent young, queer, pansexual, noncisgender crowd, as observed by Morandini, Blaszczynski, and Dar-Nimrod (2017), advances the social emancipation that began with the emergence of the homosexual subject in the twentieth century. Maybe it is a matter of taking advantage of the momentum provided by the so-called "gender revolution" to fuel the necessarily associated anti-capitalist struggle. Homonormativity (Duggan 2004, 50) and pink capitalism may accommodate the gay neoliberal subject with ease, and the queer subject is not immune to a similar process of assimilation. But, at least in its conceptual foundations, *queer* might be the adequate terrain for a proper agency of resistance, a social force that deserves to be supported.

In this joyful dynamic, the socio-material ground of this chapter comprises the confluence of three phenomena: the explosion of queerness as cultural phenomenon; a regain of interest for alternative modes of social organization and reproduction; and a resurgence of discourse around ethics of sensibility in feminist scholarship. These three markers signal a potential positive shift toward a mentality of communal living in celebration of *difference,* a tendency in which the family appears to be a privileged terrain of transformation. A kinship system is not a structure but a practice, a praxis, a method, and even a strategy (Deleuze and Guattari 2009, 167). Therefore, my attempt is to articulate queer communal kinship as a new praxis of family.

1. queer

*Queerness is a structuring and educated mode of desiring that
allows us to see and feel beyond the quagmire of the present. The
here and now is a prison house. We must strive, in the face of the
here and now's totalizing rendering of reality, to think and feel a
then and there.*

— Muñoz (2009, 1)

*A critical vantage on the social we can call queer emerges
[…] from within a century-long history of struggle against
compulsory heterosexuality, a history that itself is conditioned by
capital's internal differentiation of social relations.*

— Floyd (2009, 20)

According to the *Oxford English Dictionary,* the noun "queer"
was first used to signify "homosexual" by the Marquess of
Queensbury in 1894. The *Concise New Partridge Dictionary of
Slang* says the adjective "queer" began to mean "homosexual"
around 1914, mostly in the United States, and notes that it was
"derogatory from the outside, not from within," a hint that it was
already embraced as a self-description (Perlman 2019). Today,
"queer" is a word that can cause confusion. Sometimes used as
an umbrella term to refer to a range of sexual identities that are
deviant from the norm of heterosexuality, it is also employed
as a term that calls into question the stability of any such categories of identity based on sexual orientation. In this second
sense, "queer" signifies a critique of the tendency to organize
political or theoretical questions around sexual orientation per
se. It becomes a way to denaturalize categories such as "lesbian"
and "gay" (not to mention "straight" and "heterosexual"), revealing them as socially and historically constructed identities
(Burgett and Hendler 2020, 198).

By extending this logic, any practice transgressing current
classifications, traditional representations, or (sexual) social
norms can qualify as queer. Queer, then, appears to describe

marginal practices developing on the fringes of society. Following this foundation on a spatial metaphor of periphery, it is easy to romanticize queer as this vanguard, experimental force pushing the limits of what is possible at a certain point in time. I believe this is what José Esteban Muñoz (2009) had in mind when he wrote that "queer aesthetics map future social relations" (1). Indeed, it is important to see queer as a performative force, since it is not only a *being* but a *doing* for and toward the future — queer as ideality, a political horizon.

Presently, as an epistemology that poses for its founding axiom that people intrinsically differ, and identities are never static, queer theory brings up appreciated complications to the categories of "family," "child," "woman/man," and "motherhood/fatherhood." Queer kinship does not require these old, binary, naturalized, fixed identity positions, even though it has to, and joyfully does, deal with the ways in which they are inscribed in western culture.

Hope and enthusiasm

These two dimensions of *queer*, defying the present and imagining the future, will be discussed in the coming paragraphs. Let me start by declaring the axiomatic affect of my conceptual proposal, or the tone that I propose to associate with this political posture, that of *enthusiasm*. This principle is to be contrasted with the notion of hope, which Muñoz, following Ernst Bloch and his notion of concrete utopia, deploys in relation to "queerness", writing about hope as both a critical affect and a methodology. For Muñoz, hope provides the solution to address the latent atmosphere of political pessimism in which he sees us immersed, hope as a hermeneutic of progress.

I agree with Muñoz that political imagination is a necessary component to any strategy that aims to bypass the grim prospects offered by our current sociomaterial condition. We need to locate spaces to imagine a queer and non-capitalist future, and experiments in the aesthetic realm might provide a practical terrain to do so. However, I have a problem with the word "hope" as much as it conveys the meaning of an idealistic vision that drives social forces of change, an articulation that suspiciously resonates with theological or "progressive" types of narrative. There is also an undesirable component of passivity in hope, which somehow involves waiting for something to happen, whereas I conceive of enthusiasm as an active dynamic that generates curiosity, the driving force of the self-educated revolutionary subject. All in all, enthusiasm seems more pragmatic and engaged than hope, or optimism for that matter; a disillusioned, secular affective strategy.

Indeed, there is nothing idealistic in the type of practices that we, as queers, should look for in the present in order to imagine and shape what our desired future might be. Empathy, sensitivity, non-violence, and openness are not only idealist notions but very concrete psychosocial tendencies to defend and accentuate through political and cultural action. To frame the project of expanding queer subjectivity as idealistic is a dangerous political stance. We are dreamers because we are ambitious, not because we are lulled in illusions. Muñoz's focus on aesthetics is maybe the reason why he finds appeal in the notion of hope. In the field of art, hope can certainly be conceived as a powerful force of affective generation. But I would prefer to rely on enthusiasm on the micropolitical level, since it can build on social practices and not on artistic productions.

In that sense I diverge from the humanities in that the analytical research pursued on the theme of queerness is often too oriented towards the aesthetics of the movement, while there is a major importance in theorizing it as a sociopolitical phenomenon. Of course, the politics of representation is as important as the study of artistic forms generating aesthetic experiences that parallel or evoke the sociomaterial reality of queers' daily existence. But the tendency of certain theorists affectively driven by a fantasy to hang out with the cool artsy kids, or scholars staying within the comfort of their literary studies PhDs instead of getting their hands dirty with social reality, a phenomenon privileged by universities as bourgeois institutions, results in the danger that I can very much see emerging these days, namely that queer is neutralized as an aesthetic ideal, a movement of cosmetic change wrapped with idealist fantasies or naive statements.

I don't fundamentally disagree with Muñoz. On the contrary, I think both our conceptual articulations of queer follow the same trajectory, of a refusal of the status quo and political depression. We are surely aiming at the same objective, but our terminologies must diverge. While I'm looking for enthusiasm in the realm of social practices, and he's looking at hope in the expression of specific art forms, we both share the same aim of psychological and material benefits for the marginal and the non-normative. In my case, enthusiasm is not the methodology. It is not even the place for criticality, but it simply serves as a support to it. It might be more closely related to Michael Snediker's (2009) notion of queer optimism, which he frames as a reflexive site for meditations on the worldly conditions that would deserve optimism. Whereas Snediker's interest lies in locating positive projections in queer literary and aesthetic productions, I am more interested in defining the affective tonality of a sociopolitical engagement informed by materialist considerations.

To be precise, there are situations when enthusiasm may have to be camouflaged as hope, in the context of political representation. To garnish this argument, I would like to put in perspective affective strategies deployed by two of my personal heroes, Guillaume Dustan and Éric Fassin, first by considering the deliberate *naivety* of Dustan's public figure, in the attitude he deployed during his infamous apparitions on television (Dustan 2021, 25). Sharing his views, which were radical for that era, as if they had to be taken as completely obvious, performatively aimed for a redefinition of what should be understood as common sense. It acted as if mainstream media could follow him in his cause despite his obvious instrumentalization as a polemical figure.

Second, in a presentation entitled "Mobilizing Publics: Intellectuals, Activists, and the Political Work of Representation,"

Fassin (2015a) proposes arrogance as a political strategy to counterbalance the fact that left-wing voices are minoritarian, making them sound more numerous and powerful than they really are. This cheeky intervention, voiced in the serious context of an academic conference, reveals a concern that would certainly have been shared by Dustan, since they both seem to be reacting to a similar realization that they cannot define their modes of representation on an honest account of themselves. Although these strategies, naivety and arrogance, have their own merits and weaknesses and seem to propose two radically different registers, I believe that their common denominator is embodying enthusiasm disguised as hope. In other words, they are not hoping that a different future might come, but they performatively enact their agency as indisputable.

Indeed, if they had to represent their thinking in a truthful manner, Dustan would probably not go on television, and Fassin would have to concede that the agency of leftist intellectuals is markedly limited. For both of them, that acting against the odds of a conservative and sexist society is a difficult and partially hopeless endeavor. Therefore, it is only thanks to this shift in attitude that they still successfully manage to convey their message into the public sphere. Paradoxically, staying aligned with their ethics requires them to deviate from a strictly materialist assessment of the social in their public discourse.

In terms of long-term political strategy, I agree with Muñoz that queerness, understood as a horizon of hope, is probably one of the most exciting things happening in our cultural landscape today. As a motive occupying the mental space of young people in favor of a reformist dynamic of swapping out hate and fear for an embodied philosophy of love, care, and openness, the potential of queerness should not be considered auxiliary. This is where queer intervenes as a generator of both enthusiasm and hope, in the here and now, as much as in the there and then. Indeed, what better vehicle to generate positive affects than the exhilarating feeling of seeing queer as emerging from the history of LGBT and feminist activism and culture — what a party!

For now, let's focus on enthusiasm as an affective channel for daily, micropolitical dynamics of change. This principle is to be applied in a simple biochemical sense. Enthusiasm, far from being linked with naivety or even optimism, is simply a healthy menu to resist our living conditions in an environment highly impacted by the production of lack or libidinal repression that is inherent to a patriarcho-capitalist regime of desire. In an era of massive, industrial instrumentalization of our cognitive processes, when paranoia and frustration are capitalized to the molecular level, anger and fear are regularly enforced as the most profitable affective tonalities for circulating and producing contemporary subjectivities. In this context, the only sane and reasonable approach might be to follow a strict diet of enthusiasm, simply to not succumb to the sirens of both the dominant order of commodified depression and the idealist projection of a dreamed future. This approach can be linked with the "revolutionary nature of joy" found in the anarchist tradition, addressing the defeatism of depression while avoiding reference to a fantasized insurrection. So, enthusiasm all over the place! To that end, let me expand on my favorite conceptual character, that suspicious figure whose emergence may in fact signal the realization of a glorious and enduring philosophical agenda: the queer.

An Anti-normative Agent

> The preference for "queer" represents, among other things, an aggressive impulse of generalization; it rejects a minoritizing logic of toleration or simple political interest-representation in favor of a more thorough resistance to regimes of the normal.
>
> — Warner (1993, xxvi)

As the monster, the queer is characterized by its refusal to participate in the classificatory "order of things": a disturbing hybrid whose incoherent collective identity resists attempts to include itself in any systematic structure. Queer also resists any classification built on hierarchy or binary opposition, demanding instead a "system" allowing polyphony and polymorphism, a deeper play of difference. Indeed, the queer is difference made flesh, but not in a fixed, individualistic sense. Queer is a mindset, a personal and collective narrative, not an essence. By revealing that difference is arbitrary and potentially free-floating, mutable rather than essential, it threatens to question not just individual members of society, but the very cultural apparatus through which individuality is constituted and allowed (Cohen 2012, 12). By its active deconstruction of cultural norms, the queer as tendency or trait, seeks out society in order to demand its body's raison d'être and to bear witness to the fact that it could have been constructed otherwise.

I didn't think I was "queer" until people started telling me so. Previously, it never occurred to me that this label suited me, simply because my focus was elsewhere and that my gendersex identity didn't strike me as excessively transgressive. Therefore it is only recently, when I gave myself the chance to identify with this notion, that I started to think about labels again, since it reminded me of another one that got stamped on me, years before: the couple. A very common scheme. Two people are attracted to each other and "fall in love." They don't necessarily think about defining their status, but quickly, it's a label, a categorization that hits them. They are now a couple and are very much invited to proceed on the normal agenda of the couple society. I remember laughing about that whole scheme with a lover some years ago, until we got into the habit of being perceived as a couple and finally accepted being categorized as one.

Similarly, it is interesting that before this interpellation that pushed me into self-identifying with being "queer," I didn't have much interest in the concept. There was therefore a performative efficacy in the act of labeling me, as it led me into a quest to understand the reasons behind this interpellation and to educate myself on the topic of queerness, in the same way that being called a "couple" had generated for me a reflection on this topic, because in both cases the identification was not self-initiated. As much as these events raise spaces for self-reflection, they also create conditions for normalization that go against the principle of radical difference.

Resisting Labels

Queer is under threat of constant reterritorialization through the application of labels. Labels are part of the normative apparatus and are projected on its constitutive outside repeatedly in a process of absorption. This is manifest in relational practices, especially the ones that interest us. If one simply steps outside of the couple-form and into the unknown, they will quickly be labeled as polyamorous; if one feels attracted to the whole spectrum of gender expression, they might quickly be constrained in the reductive label of bisexuality. Once the label is internalized, the subject loses its agency over its initial commitment to the larger field of possibilities. That is where the notion of queer comes in as a handy, potentially disruptive labelling tool, that is, the label of the anti-label.

Queer resists its self-inscription into labels, inventing situated modes of living. Thus, it comes from the privileged position that rejects the social confirmation associated with the usual process of labeling. This is a limiting factor for my utopian character. As much as the queer is made fragile by its normative environment, most often to the level of trauma, they still emerge from an initial privileged subject position for whom queerness is a historically available and affordable option, compared to the one who has "fallen" into normalization. Notably, in *Bodies That Matter,* Judith Butler warns us to ask ourselves for whom does the term present an impossible conflict between racial, ethnic, or religious affiliation and sexual politics (2011, 173). She advocates for the necessity of a genealogical critique of the queer subject. This is where materialist feminism comes in as a necessary section in the queer curriculum.

Queer Is the Substance

Whereas *communal* is its practical elaboration, and *kinship* its strategic orientation, queer is the substantive component of my conceptual articulation. Queer is also prospective, following the definition of queerness as horizon developed by Muñoz, a set of indicators looking forward to future fulfillment. In that sense, it is set in opposition to the recursive temporal aspect of narratives of social change that rely on a pre-intelligible unfolding, wherein the role of its actors is worked out backward from its conceived ends. The orthodox marxist revolutionary program is a good example of this type of narrative construct. Uri Gordon (2018) shows us how this retrospective mode is often imbued within a theological tradition. On the one hand, this type of narrative allures by its reassuring programmatic stability, while queer, on the other hand, strives on instability and calls for constant rearticulation. The experimental nature of lived ethics undercuts recursive reasoning.

Queer is an anti-repression machine that successfully actualizes its potential, but not without tension. In that process, it has to grieve the rest of us and the parts of itself that succumbed to normativity. In that sense, queer is stuck in a constant mourning of society, that complements its celebration of the joy of difference. Of course, this is the idealization of a concept. Any critical observer will notice the layer of normalization in the expansion of queerness as a social movement. Queer is not the solution to save the world, as it is imbued in identity politics that clouds the materialist implications of redistributive justice for its demography. But, as a traveling anti-normative incentive, a generative keyword, it carries the potential for change that any scholar of difference should get excited about, but only, maybe, if we allocate it this power with performative enthusiasm.

To be clear, problematizing identity politics is thinking of it in terms of usefulness (my activist credo): if identity is something to explore and learn from, to trigger processes of becoming, collective formations, or epistemic shifts, then it can be useful. If it becomes a form of conformism, feeding essentialist and idealist beliefs that obfuscate some aspects of reality, then it can be dangerous. Of course, it is never simply one way or the other, because we are all driven by idealist, mental constructions in our daily actions. This is about the pleasure we get from life in the certainty of our actions, in the same way that addicts learn

to balance their addiction with the other parts of their existence. (Deleuze speaks of the penultimate glass of the alcoholic
[Boutang, Deleuze, and Parnet 2004].) Queer, as an identity that
warns against identities or our addiction to idealist identifica-
tions, can be a useful tool.

As Michel Foucault once said:

> [I]f we are asked to relate to the question of identity, it must
> be an identity to our unique selves. But the relationships we
> have to have with ourselves are not ones of identity; rather,
> they must be relationships of differentiation, of creation, of
> innovation. To be the same is really boring. We must not
> exclude identity if people find their pleasure through this
> identity, but we must not think of this identity as an ethical
> universal rule. (2000, 166)

What he envisions is a society of tolerance in which everyone
can be themselves while still maintaining a functioning social
order. Is this the shout of a utopian dream, or the harbinger of
an individualist nightmare? To get a better sense, we need to
understand what he means by differentiation, or difference.

Rehabilitating Difference

In his work *Difference and Repetition,* Deleuze (1994) attempts
to free the concept of difference from its dialectical position
for which all change is considered relative, and all critique to
be responsive. Difference is then not subject to "identity in the
concept, opposition in the predicate, analogy in judgment and
resemblance in perception" (262). Moving away from this four-
fold principle of reason, which remains faithful to the principle
of representation, Deleuze offers us a difference that is not a secondary principle, as in "consequential to something" (Braidotti
and Dolphijn 2014, 14). In doing so, he attempts to rehabilitate
difference from its negative charge resulting from our European
history of colonialism and fascism, as well as major strands of

historical, western philosophy. As summarized by Rosi Braidotti and Rick Dolphijn:

> The equation of difference with pejoration, as a term that indexes exclusion from the entitlements to subjectivity, is built into the tradition which defines the Subject as coinciding with/being the same as consciousness, rationality, and self-regulating ethical behavior. This results in making entire sections of living beings into marginal and disposable bodies: these are the sexualized, racialized and naturalized others. (29)

Therefore, what this philosophy of difference does is stressing the need to elaborate forms of social and political implementation of non-pejorative and non-dualistic notions of "others" (Braidotti 2006, 76).

This is the type of difference for which the queer bears allegiance in my conceptual formation. Understood as a conceptual character, queer is the flag-bearer of difference, its advocate, and its worker. As a critical practitioner, queer engages in practices of creative affirmation, distancing from the logic of negativity and pursuing the joyful production of transformative political acts. This is where I locate queer enthusiasm, that is, in the practice of a political subjectivity focused on becoming, which desires the self as a process of transformation untied from the knots of reactionary, negatively articulated desire.

This principle serves as the basis for the development of an ethics of a non-oppositional political imagination, and the desire to activate the thinking of radical difference. "There is no logical necessity to link political subjectivity to oppositional consciousness and reduce critique to negativity" (Braidotti and Dolphijn 2014, 26), which is what happens so often when crowds of leftist thinkers gather to articulate the sharpest definition of the latest attire of capital. This is something that people accustomed to large-scale intellectual and academic gatherings will easily recognize, that is, the number of resources spent on producing a flood of discourse, of impressive rigor and precision, that still result in a gross lack of political imagination, reducing these events to mere networking festivities.

In opposition to this, queer and *queer communal kinship* (QCK) are the search for conditions that may facilitate the understanding of "difference in itself" as an affirmative praxis or an "art of living" dedicated to the liberation of our desires from the patriarcho-capitalist machinery. The label "queer" is associated with an affective investment in the identification as nonnormative, or in opposition to hetero- and homonormativity. It might seem that this process of becoming-other through the deconstruction of normative identities is a requirement to ground the work of radical difference. It also leads us to the pressing question of understanding what these notions of the "normal" or "normative" actually mean.

The cost of normalcy

Let's expand a bit on this question of anti-normativity, because it is thrown into every sauce these days. Maybe we must refrain from an overly romantic investment in this notion. What is normal anyway? The term only entered everyday speech in the mid-twentieth century (Cryle and Stephens 2017). Before that, it was solely a scientific term used primarily in medicine to refer to a general state of health and the orderly function of organs. The statistical notion of normality appeared at the end of the nineteenth century in the work of Francis Galton who simultaneously developed the notion of eugenics. Note that Galton was the cousin of dear Charles Darwin, a detail that reminds us how much the influence of the few, or the very localized action of some old white men, permeates our culture and our understanding of reality.

So, normality is yet another modern, patriarcho-colonial concept. What to make out of it in relation to family? And what about queer? Is it a vain form of resistance, a self-interested movement without any potential of supporting dynamics of cross-class sensibility and redistribution? This may be partially true, but it is also quite far from the whole story. What interests me behind this conceptual character's providential agency is the affective sense of solidarity that might come through a collective detachment from the normative world.

In her book *Cruel Optimism,* Lauren Berlant argues that normality, as this fantasy to which we attach ourselves, this fantasy of the "good life," is a mental construct detrimental or counterproductive to our happiness. This attachment is what she calls "a relation of cruel optimism," which "exists when something you desire is actually an obstacle to your flourishing" (2011, 1). In that framing, the normative good life supposed to reward obedience to the rules of society works as the index of projected happiness, the illusional investment in a future that is already canceled. In the case that interests us, it is this fantasy of a happy, heteronormative family that can be unwrapped following Berlant's reflection.

This is especially relevant when a spreading precarity provides the dominant experience of the moment, an affective atmosphere penetrating most social classes and exemplified with this emerging social group conceptualized as the *precariat.* While the social-democratic promise of the postwar period in the United States and Europe has vanished into an old dream, people have remained attached to its fantasies of a secured existence that neoliberalism has rendered elusive. In this context, we might understand the permanent state of "crisis" under which we are subjugated as an affect that naturalizes the intensification of exploitation. Expectations of upward mobility, job security, political and social equality, and durable intimacy — taken for granted and shaping the rhythm of life associated with the bourgeois family model — don't apply anymore, even for the social stratum most accustomed to these givens that we nowadays call the middle class.

This may result in a major transformation that promises to shake the social order of our society. The scripted life of the western bourgeois family model, which may have always been dysfunctional for most but perfectly suited the middle-class existence, is becoming unadapted, unsuitable for all of us. As a result, middle-class people (which, let's be honest, will probably

or sexuality. As this might make my appropriation of the voices of feminist and queer thinkers to shape my own story suspect, a brief clarification may be useful here.

There has been a semantic shift around the term "queer," following the decades in which its meaning has evolved from a pre-reclaimed, essentialist judgment of sexual preference and monstrosity toward a cultural and gender-troubling notion of identity. Nowadays, at least in some European militant circles, this word is associated with an anti-essentialist and anti-authoritarian stature, encompassing a post-colonial, post-gender, and neurodiverse understanding of subjectivity and embodiment. Therefore, I endorse a strategic operationalization of the term "queer" as the conflation of an identity shaped by a contingent set of relational practices, including gender performativity and sexuality, and a consciously shared, overtly anti-capitalist political positioning: we are *queer*, not *queers*.

This is not at all a new strategy. In the old days of the gay liberation movement, there was some debate around the term "gay," whether to think of it as an individual sexual preference or as an "embattled identity" (Bettocchi 2021, 80), an anti-heteronormative political positioning distanced from a mere essentialist or cultural identification. This politicization of the terms "gay" and "queer" challenges the dominant psychoanalytic model that locates a person within a sexualized subjectivity, a model that has been central to many of the modern narratives and norms that organize personal and institutional life (Berlant 2012, 15).

Nevertheless, it is important not to de-sexualize queerness as this is one of the sites of deconstruction par excellence. Even though asexuality is very much part of queer culture, we need to compose with what we have, that is, where we come from, a cultural context that links sexuality with identity. In that regard, self-identification with queerness offers the potential to detach from the framework of thought that solidifies a naturalized family order. Indeed, it is from the western sexual cosmology that the naturalized roles of "mother," "father," "son," and "daughter" are derived. I scrutinize queer collectivity here in order to locate emancipatory social practices that result not from a sexual otherness, but as a possibility embedded in the break from heteronormative life narratives (Halberstam 2011, 70). Another study may have looked at the ways in which queerness more directly disrupts or subverts heteronormative identity models through sexuality, for example when the father–son model of obedience and stability is turned into a daddy–boy relationship sexualizing generational difference (73).

Indeed, queer suggests a culture in which sexuality is more closely related to pleasure than to romantic love or reproduction, one in which sexual fulfillment would be seen as healthy, diverse, and joyous, detached from its patriarcho-romantic symbolic overweight. Furthermore, the notion of sexual identity, troubled by the queer subject, is challenged in its usual characteristics of permanency, stability, fixity, and near impermeability to change. Queer thus resists the kind of assimilation that happens for example with the naturalized homosexual subject, with all the dangers that such a process represents. Unlike the western version of the subject conceived as unitary, authentic, bounded, static, and trans-situational, a queer framework of identity makes it possible to imagine a self conceptualized as "multiplicitous, malleable, dynamic, contextually salient" (Wekker 1999, 125).

Therefore, in the same way that I believe the fight against patriarchy beneficially impacts any gendered human creature on this planet, I would say that queer is for everyone, if one considers the acceptance of a post-gender social order as something prefiguratively attained. In a sense, it's a conscious performative gesture. We need to create spaces where this fight is achieved, as it shall be in the future — if my readers will allow me this small deviation into the realm of hope. It is in the same vein that Maria Lugones (2007), in her elaboration of what she calls the "colonial/modern gender system," writes, "we need to place ourselves in a position to call each other to reject this gender system as we perform a transformation of communal relations" (189). Note the introduction of the notion of "communal" and the idea of placing ourselves collectively in a certain setting. This book, and that is part of its utopian character, is trying to be one of these "safe spaces," in which a binary epistemology of gender and naturalized visions of race and sexuality would be complete anachronisms, residues from the past that we can look back at with a slight embarrassment and move on.

Of course, this approach risks putting aside the very concrete issues at stake with current gender dynamics in the world. The celebratory tone in which I write could also easily lead to the dark territory of queer exceptionalism, in which one blinds themself with the idea that queer people are free from the rampant racism, sexism, ableism, and ageism that can be found in the straight society. There is some performative, strategic idealism in these lines that aims to be generative of enthusiasm but should not refrain one from criticality. So, what I can say is this: don't be afraid to call yourself "queer"! Don't take it as a label (or use it as a label to start questioning labels) but as an incentive to look for difference and processes of becoming in your relational practices. Again, as a horizon for yourself, for humanity, for the world. A warm feeling of connection. Deconstructing gender roles, but also individualism, accumulation, or competition, are practices that can be intimidating in our current culture but much easier to perform when you feel legitimate to do so. Use the power of words. Queer is for everyone!

2. communal

While the planet is getting warmer, the democratic pact is freezing. That seems logical. Freezing allows one to block out a scary experience that may be too difficult to process. Freezing releases endorphins, calming the body and relieving pain. This is what happens when we confine ourselves and shop online instead of overthrowing our corrupt governments. This is what happens when we endlessly talk about a virus and its different commercial vaccines as if we all suddenly became amateur epidemiologists, instead of talking about how it is possible that democracy worldwide has vanished to such levels of farce and desolation.

Communal resists the political strategies of fear and psychosocial repression deployed by our political rulers, as enmeshed as they are with the greedy forces of cognitive capitalism and our corporate moguls. Fear freezes, whereas communal grooves. It is not a shallow nor foolish thing to say that we will have to dance our way out of capitalism. *Are these words dancing enough?* Remember that the rhythm of capital escalates in accumulation (ideology of growth), aiming for climax (profit), whereas communal indulges in the pleasures of nonlinearity (debunking progress), asynchronous patterns (generative agonism), and textural delay (degrowth). That's why capitalism makes bad sex and tall buildings, phallocentrism and premature ejaculations, whereas communal promises us orgies that would put shame on Michelangelo Antonioni's *Zabriskie Point.* Again, it's the groove that matters.

More seriously, communal is about asking the real questions: how do we organize, in terms of time and space? How do we share resources and work? How do we make decisions? More precisely, communal is about the "collectivization of reproductive labor and consumption, the abolition of the family, and the freeing of love, care and eroticism into a collective, democratic space of shared life" (O'Brien 2019).

A catastrophic communication campaign

It all comes out as the result of a confusion, which obviously has been, to a certain extent, orchestrated — bring out your conspiracy theories! — but one reason why old white men in boring business suits are still running the world for the most part is simply because the other options have received the most terrible advertising campaigns that could have been imagined. Look.

Competition? Sweat and muscles, very sexy. Accumulation? Gold bars and shiny phallic towers, very bling-bling. These are the principles of capitalism, fueled by its appealing iconography of opulence and domination. Now what about communal? If talking about communism, old decaying concrete towers from the Soviet era? About communes, fucking mandalas, dirt, some lukewarm, watery soup? How is that supposed to make one leave the comfort of their Netflix homes? Where is the amazing imagery of communal to push forward its principles of collectivity, inclusivity, and sharing? What we are dealing with is a deep, long lasting advertising issue. The faces of communal are desperately dull and very not sexy. We need some serious representational politics of pleasure to address this emergency.

Indeed, who is talking about communal living? Smelly permaculture nerds or well-intentioned but dead-boring straight scholars. That's one of my aims for this book: to motivate my fellow queers to take over and occupy that discursive space. We need to queer the commune — make it sexy, flashy, viral. Performatively *hot* — Savage Ranch style (Love Bailey 2018). Queers are often already communal by association. They have to collectivize and share to survive this ugly world full of violence for the outsiders to "the norm" (or did I read too much Judith Butler?). They — I'm talking about those who can afford it — just need to push this already fundamental aspect of their existence to the front.

intentional communities

From nineteenth-century anarchist communities to the hippie communes of the 1960s, communal living emerges as a long-standing and, at least today, well-documented tradition. The umbrella term that seems to have established itself in academic research, "intentional communities," leads to approximately 12,100 results on a search engine of academic references. My goal here is not to dive into any historical study, but to try to establish what defines a communal "spirit" or philosophy and how its concrete and conscious application can support a gradual detachment from capitalist patterns of relation.

In his study *The 60s Communes: Hippies and Beyond,* Timothy Miller distinguishes a series of criteria for him to formulate a definition of intentional communities: a sense of common purpose and of separation from the dominant society; some form and level of self-denial in favor of the good of the group;

geographic proximity; regular personal interaction; economic sharing; a real and concrete existence; and finally, what he calls "critical mass," arbitrarily setting this threshold at "at least five individuals, some of whom must be unrelated by biology or by exclusive intimate relationship" (1999, xxii). This last point is of relevant interest, since Miller explicitly states that he excludes families (nuclear or extended) from the notion of community.

This leads us to what is certainly the main fragility or ambiguity in my articulation of queer communal kinship and also its main potential of generative conceptual friction, that is, the association of the two terms, *communal* and *kinship*, and the paradox this proposition induces. This is what is at stake when Elizabeth Freeman questions the fact that any genuinely democratic culture may perhaps need to abandon the notion of kinship (2008, 297). As a conceptual tool that discerns affective units of focused care and attention, kinship seems to necessarily have an exclusionary dimension when it is confronted with the notion of community. Like family, kinship makes a distinction between those who are "inside," and the others. Moreover, the abstract notion of community as a larger social formation is often subconsciously modeled on the liberal nation and mobilized by segregational politics of disputable agendas.

On the other hand, I would argue that queer intentional communities, be they in their idealized version exempted from the naturalized order of things as applied in biogenetic families, blur the lines between kinship and community. When you start queering kinship and community you necessarily arrive at some sort of hybrid, and it is this step away from normative generationality that interests me in its potential to articulate an organization of the social that erases patterns of exclusion, hence the necessary association of communal and kinship in one same conceptual formation. This is not a new idea as this resonates with the marxist concept of *Gemeinwesen* or real community.

capital love or communal desire?

> *In place of the individual and egoistic family, a great universal*
> *family of workers will develop, in which all the workers, men*
> *and women, will above all be comrades. This is what relations*
> *between men and women in the communist society will be like.*
> *These new relations will ensure for humanity all the joys of a love*
> *unknown in the commercial society of capitalism.*
>
> —Kollontai (1984, 16)

In my conceptual melting pot, while *queer* was relying partly on anarchist theories of affection, *communal* should logically look to similar inquiries from the communist side. Since I am one of these leftist youngsters who is too lazy to even glance at Karl Marx's heavy tomes of *Capital* and thinks *The Origin of the Family* smells a bit outdated, I will help myself with a recently published book by Richard Gilman-Opalsky (2020), *The Communism of Love.* While suspiciously conservative in some ways, definitely not queer and written in this self-sufficient tone (with royal "we" and everything) making me worried that my feminist transition made me incapable of reading most cis-men's writings, the book points at the main issue at stake in shaping what I define as communal: the pervasiveness of liberal individualism and its stubborn grip on our thinking in late capitalism. To develop a real collective subject that is not secondary to the individual, we need to look for a collectivity formed in our non-capitalist being-in-the-world, our relations to other human beings that maintain a sociality beyond and against exchange relations.

In communist slang, this is exemplified by the word "comrade," which performatively enacts a sort of universal kinship. This is where the communist ideology challenges the family model we have in the west, as Alexandra Kollontai famously put it in her 1920 pamphlet *Communism and the Family.* More recently, Jodi Dean's *Comrade: An Essay on Political Belonging* (2019) takes on the term's history and develops the story of communist comradeship as a relationship characterized by discipline, joy, courage, and enthusiasm, something that resonates somehow with my articulation of queer as an affective force. However, "comrade" summons more clearly notions of equality and solidarity, but it also conveys a sense of uniformity, a certain "sameness" provided by the romanticization of the political class struggle and the revolutionary horizon of communism. Therefore, inasmuch as Dean's thesis is valid when she shows that the shift from "comrades" toward "allies" in leftist address might be the semantic indicator of a turn toward individualism in our conception of solidarity, the uniforming aspect of "comrade" might make it unadapted to convey a force of leftist identification in our twenty-first century, since it still wears stigmas associated with totalitarianism. As a potential alternative to express our shared worldly condition, I could cite Haraway's fleshly proposition of "companion": "We are companions, *cum panis,* at table together" (2016a, 215).

So what then do we mean by "love," which, for Gilman-Opalsky, is a sort of communist relationality? Is this what resides behind this concept of the communal that I am trying to shape, a sort of affective internationalism? While we are at it, could we make it post-human, please? Okay, *why not.* How to find out? There are as many definitions of love out there as there are self-appointed philosophers. The question is what do we do with this concept; how does it work; is it *useful*? Unfortunately, what Gilman-Opalsky's book reveals is the romantic engagement with the concept that lies behind its use by the author. Statements like "human aspiration to love expresses a longing for a form of communist relationality" (2020, 5) or "love is necessarily anticapitalist" (173) are cute but highly idealistic and not necessarily grounded in contemporary or feminist ethics. Far from a materialist philosophical engagement with reality, they reveal the blind investment of their author into his favored ideology.

Indeed, any open eye in this world can observe how the notion of love is largely conflated with capitalist desire. An attempt to pretend otherwise is, at best, poetry, at worse theoretical delusion. It takes quite a leap of faith to believe that the concept of "love," as it is currently intricated in all sorts of capitalist flows of desire, has a chance to serve a present communist agenda. In terms of material semiotics, that would simply be a mistake, an inevitable failure. To say that what people experience on a daily basis — love in a propertarian sense — is not "true love" would be to negate the very real lived intensity of love under capital as experienced by many.

Additionally, I would argue that "love" can be sold, for sure, when it materializes in a commodity, which is not a bad thing in itself. To my understanding, commodities are now very much part of the world, and refuting them on principle would be absurd. As a mode of exchange, the commodity-form has shown to be quite convenient. The problem is the totalization of money overcoding everything through capitalist assimilation, not money itself. In that sense, Gilman-Opalsky's argument that the "processed-food industry will never make the best and freshest foods" (14) is not entirely relevant in a social landscape where restaurants can produce the highest quality of products. If anything, food is not the right example to argue against the fact that money can pretty much buy everything. This, and that "[k]itchens of all kinds everywhere on earth are full of families cooking for and feeding one another" are forms of sentimentalism for the private, cozy refuge of the family keeping us sane and safe from the evil, capitalist world outside.

To clarify what I mean by commodities containing "love," an example might be bands selling merch after their concerts. Indeed, most musicians don't make a decent living by selling or performing their music, so merchandising is often a way to signify personal support in a practical and symbolic way through the direct exchange of cash with an object. While usually entangled in complex, global capitalist webs of production, what these commodities can produce is loving transactions between artists and their audience. Many of us will recall such an event. For me, I would think of the hand-printed bag I bought from Sateen in New York after their performance at the Dreamhouse in 2017, a process that involved both a bunch of dollar bills and a joyful bodily interaction, an exchange of affection and human connection that I assume went both ways. And in the years after that, as I was proudly rocking this bag in my daily commutes, the object became a part of me, of my identity, inscribed in a narrative of belonging — isn't that what love is about?

So, to attempt the transformation of love through non-capitalist appropriations of the notion or literary meditations on the concept is a legitimate and important endeavor. Gilman-Opalsky himself writes, "we cannot allow bourgeois romanticism to claim love" (180) — for sure, but to conceptually rely on it for shaping a political discourse without falling into some sort of conservatism seems highly optimistic. This also neglects the fact that what love is most deeply inscribed in, where it mostly comes from in discourse, is religion, and theological narratives of illusory promises custom-made for domination. So, let's not waste too much time on that word, "love." Since I'm here looking for an activist (i.e., useful) engagement with theory, it seems to me that the concept is the holder of too much confusion. Love is not what it's all about.

What about communal, then? It is quite simple: communal is the affective attachment in distancing oneself from the dominant logic of private self-interest. It is about the pleasure to be found in non-objectified relations. It is about, once again, an enthusiastic engagement in experimentation, one could even say an egoistic self-satisfying dynamic of stepping away from capitalism, the joyful celebration of a daring bet. In that process, refusing to turn collectively to normative family units of consumerist activity seems obviously like the way to go. Seriously, let's try anything but that. Furthermore, communal is about the conscious quest for relationality that escapes utilitarian calculation. Most importantly, it is about shaping the material conditions for such practices to flourish.

So, even though I don't buy this narrative of an essentialist conception of love, a universal inclination that would have been colonized by capitalist desire, Gilman-Opalsky's description of love as a communist force is still relevant, as his research provides an excellent overview of capitalist desire and some fruitful meditations on a communist alternative pathway. After all, contrary to me, he is a serious theorist and a knowledgeable marx-ist. So let's see what we can reap from his hard work.

The main point developed in this book is that capitalist logics permeate all our relations, with which I fully concur. To support this claim, Gilman-Opalsky bases his argument on the work of a series of intellectuals, which I will summarily review below.

The first one is Erich Fromm, who essentially writes in *The Sane Society* (1955) that capitalism creates insanity by promoting alienation, and that this insanity gives rise to isolation, loneli-ness, anxiety, and unhappiness, yet we have come to defend it (remember *Cruel Optimism*?). This insanity is then regarded as rational, since every social and political regime depends on a hegemonic belief in its own rationality (Gilman-Opalsky 2020, 155).

This leads us to a social regime reduced to a facade of self-in-terested exchange relations (161), since everything and thus eve-rybody is turned into a commodity. Capitalism shapes human values, "shifting us toward *things* and *having* as opposed to *peo-ple* and *being*" (172). Well, no big news so far. The problem is that Fromm, also romantically invested in his epic mission of solving the world's future, thinks that the solution is "love," something characterized by care, responsibility, respect, and knowledge (170). Since Fromm sees capitalism as immoral, there must be a moral, and this moral is "love." Blearhp.

Axel Honneth defends the idea of socialism as the practice of "becoming-social" in an increasingly alienated world by invent-ing new forms of relational practices. Honneth writes, "with the romantic idea of love a utopian vanishing point emerged that allowed members of society increasingly subject to economic pressures to preserve the vision of an emotional transcendence of day-to-day instrumentalism" (2012, 170). This is to say that capitalist subjects often feel that the only escape from this world of hyper-commodification is romantic love, even though it pro-vides absolutely no solution to any social or political problem. And this is an extremely important point, as it tackles what he coins "romantic individualism," this ideology of opposing pri-vate romantic love to capitalism which was "probably always a typical product of bourgeois illusion" (179), since what norma-tive couple relationships lead to is to a large extent consumerist complacency. Indeed, Honneth pursues Fromm's thesis by in-sisting on the generalization of a logic of economic rationality that he sees as the "spirit" of capitalism penetrating the capillar-ies of intimate relationships.

This resonates with my previous thought on the re-eroticiza-tion of the world, or how we need to find a path toward a distan-ciation from the narrative of romantic love as a "good enough" consolation prize to endure a capitalist existence. Breaking the illusion that our focus on private love relations can actually al-low us not to engage frontally with our pressing political issues, re-eroticizing the world actually entails its partial disenchant-ment. It also requires thinking collectively, Honneth astutely observes. He laments that "psychoanalysis is dominated by a negative image of the group" (2012, 202), revealing indeed the individualistic consequences of this hegemonic paradigm of psychological cure. If anything, psychoanalysis is part of this dynamic of social atomization since it very much rests on this idea of individuals as self-contained entities.

Moreover, psychoanalysis reinforces the hegemonic logic of association between self-construction and transactional rela-tionality. As a bourgeois social practice shaped under a capitalist economy, it inscribes an entire system of economic–monetary dependences at the heart of the desire of every subject it treats (Deleuze and Guattari 1972, 288). In a cynical way, we could say that psychoanalysts capitalize on this romantic love bullshit and thus have no interest in changing that status quo. Love is the business of psychoanalysis. Therefore, an important communal challenge is to explore alternative paradigms to this dominant individualist framework of psychological care, which would re-quire the development of transindividual, or ecological, thera-peutic methodologies. Systemic psychotherapy is perhaps a step in that direction (Barbetta, Cavagnis, and Krause 2022).

priming the communal

Gilman-Opalsky also discusses John Cacioppo, an American researcher in psychology who co-founded the field of social neuroscience. Cacioppo's contribution is essential since it tackles what may result from a dialectical opposite to my concept of communal, that is, mental loneliness. Note that this is not even about social isolation per se but the feeling of loneliness, which can be experienced while being surrounded with people. This is an alarming and generalizing phenomenon (Griffin 2010; Demarinis 2020) that can be attributed to capitalist alienation and the impoverishment of social relations when they are reduced to economic self-interested interactions as Honneth has shown us. Indeed, Cacioppo identifies American-style capitalism as the reconfiguring of a global culture of disconnection, of aggressive individualism. This is why, he urges us, a "landscape built for disconnection simply makes it even more urgent to work consciously and deliberately to build stronger human bonds at every opportunity, in very day-to-day exchange" (2008, 255). This is exactly what communal is about.

Finally, this leads us to the most important point, which is the notion of "priming," a method of conditioning that works by implanting presuppositions and activating tendencies in an open situation of encounter (Manning and Massumi 2014, 29; Massumi 2015). On this topic, Cacioppo writes:

> Money appears to have a positive impact on people's motivation, but a negative impact on their behavior toward others. There are data to suggest that merely having money on the periphery of consciousness is sufficient to skew us away from prosocial behavior. The psychologist Kathleen Vohs and her colleagues did a series of nine experiments that primed certain participants with thoughts of money. [...] In all nine tests, those who were given the subtle suggestions of money were not only less likely to ask for help, but also less likely to help others. When a lab assistant staged an accident by drop-

ping a box of pencils, those primed with thoughts of money picked up fewer. (2008, 264–65)

The reason of my emphasis on this concept of the communal is really to insist on the importance of dealing with the individual-istic conditioning that is now deeply rooted in our western psy-che as a result of generations of life under capitalism. Not only do we have to develop alternative narratives to capitalist self-accomplishment, we also need to strategically disperse primings of communal desire, as affective triggers to the emotional ap-propriation of these alternative narratives.

It is not easy to deal with the pervasiveness of money invading our psyches to the point of becoming omnipresent, channeling any of our emotional drives through the filtering of its own cod-ing. The logic of turning everything into capital happens in each and every one of us in a granular way, subconsciously. This is what needs to be counteracted, in the molecular factory of mic-ropolitics. What we are facing is a design issue, a reality that we have to deal with. If we don't start priming ourselves with non-capitalist affects, we are definitely in trouble. Communal, like communism, is basically about un-learning money. What more exquisite idea than this?

emerging patterns of sensibility

How does communal, laid out here as a space of non-capitalist priming, emerge in an urban, integrated capitalist social field characterized by profound individualism, desensitized patri-archal subjectivity, and erratic anomie? Of course, this focus is influenced by my own personal history and conditioned by my direct access to relevant spaces of practice and discourse. For a lively account of recent experiments in rural and semi-rural environments, one might look at the road movie and book *Les sentiers de l'utopie* by Isabelle Frémeaux and John Jordan (2012), a duo of researchers who traveled Europe in search of anti-cap-italist intentional communities. What this document reveals is the importance of initiatives that seek to make-world at a different scale and in temporalities that resist those of global modernity. However, it also points at some weaknesses of intentional communities in that they are often exclusionary, hard to access, and resistant to change.

Thus the need to seek where communal patterns of relation emerge in integration to the current, mainstream social fabric and to foster these sites of emergence. It is important to locate affective investments in such dynamics inside social formations in order to identify spaces of virtual intensity. For example, it might be unrealistic and counterproductive to develop a strategy focused on the collectivization of food production in any short or middle term. Look at the average affective landscape of urban teenagers: do they rave about salads? Come on, it's much easier to just rely on monocrop industrial agriculture combined with outsourced greenhouse neo-colonial labor for our food supply and move on. That's not the narrative we need to push a collectivist agenda in the mind of urban youngsters — at least not the central one.

Without fantasizing about an insurrectional shift as a movement led by a romanticized proletariat that would allow a postcapitalist regime to flourish, it seems more urgent to strategize the types of social experiments that can be implemented in the current material setting of society, as forces of change integrated in the cultural landscape, and critically positioned (i.e., not in a blind refusal) with regard to capitalist society and the global economy. In that sense, what I advocate for is an activist mode of speculation and praxis in opposition to the — wonderful and otherwise needed — literary dreams of revolution, specifically through prefigurative politics, concrete utopia, and heterotopia.

prefigurative politics

Communal prefigures non-capitalist modes of relation. "Prefigurative politics" is a method of pursuing social change through "disengagement and reconstruction, rather than by reform or revolution" (Day 2011, 113), as a means to gradually build a new and better society "in the shell of the old" (95). Indebted to the anarchist tradition, it is an ethical revolutionary practice which fights domination by directly constructing alternatives, counter-hegemonic institutions, and modes of interaction that embody the desired transformation (Yates 2015).

Carl Boggs, credited with coining the term, has defined pre-figuration as "the embodiment, within the ongoing political practice of a movement, of those forms of social relations, de-cision-making, culture, and human experience that are the ul-timate goal" (1978, 2). According to him, three principles guide prefigurative traditions: rejection of hierarchy, disregard for political organizations with rigid and centralized power struc-tures that (re)produce power imbalances, and a "commitment to democratization through local, collective structures that antici-pate the future liberated society" (5).

Prefigurative spaces are laboratories of social change because prefigurative efforts involve recognizing and shifting power im-balances within social relationships. In my conceptual assem-blage, communal is the force that translates this principle into the material or spatiotemporal dimensions of everyday life. In the insistent affirmation of possibility that lies in the social fab-ric in which it inscribes itself, it actualizes conditions of conta-gion, emulation, and resonance. In that sense, it is important that communal aims to be open, receptive, and visible rather than insular and isolated (Trott 2016, 275).

In practice, to develop a political project of prefiguration implies a continual process of daily implementation, internal struggle, and an endless cycle of learning and adaptation (270). The struggle for social change is not an event looming on the horizon but an ongoing process.

Contrary to the conventional understanding of social move-ments as organizations with the primary objective of policy change, prefigurative politics is more concerned in shifting mentalities, beliefs, and drives that rhythmize the psychosocial fabric of society. This has been the legitimate source of criticism since it is indeed sort of impossible to know if the sole existence of prefigurative political acts will inspire their gradual spreading in the shell of a capitalist society. Nonetheless, it aligns with the program of a (micro-)politics of desire, an engagement which should be complementary to more direct political demands. I would argue that it might not be enough, but without such a pursuit, there is very little chance that things will go right.

concrete utopias

The concept of "concrete utopia" developed by Bloch (2016), which seeks to read in the present the possible that lies within it, is also relevant here. One can see how this concept completes and feeds the dynamic of prefigurative politics. When both concepts are used in combination for the development of an experimental social practice, concrete utopia is the self-reflective dimension that opens the space to formulate a pragmatic speculative orientation. This is why utopian thinking is in no way to be put in opposition to revolutionary politics. It is about what Bloch called "anticipatory consciousness," that is, a consciousness of possibilities that have not yet been, but could eventually be, realized (Bammer 2015, 3).

In recent years, this notion of concrete utopia has been extensively employed, notably in political, artistic, and academic discourse. Depending on whether one takes a masculinist (liberal) or feminist (communal?) perspective — not to essentialize anyone, but from the standpoint of a western cosmology — the battlefield for the future, or the longing for difference in the realm of the social, seems to intensify. This usage of the terminology to describe social practices seem to reveal two risky inclinations. The first is a desperate, uninformed investment into a messianic or demiurgic type of narrative, predominantly in politics; the second, a neoliberal churning of variations masquerading behind the nostalgic investment into a lost horizon of hope, predominantly in the arts. In both cases, we witness retrograde engagements in which nothing is actually concrete nor utopian. This is one of the dangers behind the allure of a programmatic engagement. For that reason, concrete utopia, as a conceptual tool, should only be employed as a practice of localization, a scouting methodology in the articulation of social practices of change, while alerting us on the dangers of idealization.

Muñoz is inspired by Bloch's notion of concrete utopia to develop his conception of queerness as horizon in his study of queer art surrounding the Stonewall period. This approach outlines "the anticipatory illumination of art, which can be characterized as the process of identifying certain properties that can be detected in representational practices helping us to see the not-yet-conscious" (2009, 3). Unraveling the not-yet-conscious is also what is at stake in my own appropriation of the concept, this time not centered on a study of aesthetics but transposed onto a political ethnographic concern. I am interested in locating concrete utopias in current anti-normative social practices in order to articulate strategies of prefigurative politics, which I will return to below.

The Communal Heterotopia

Why do privileged, white youngsters listen to rap music? To answer this question, we may want to help ourselves to the concept of "heterotopia" developed by Foucault (1984), as a place of emancipation, contestation, and invention, creating the space that does not exist within the normative (Nal 2015). In order to grasp this phenomenon of bourgeois individuals consuming cultural products emerging from lower-class culture, we must consider what is fundamentally a double process of capitalist assimilation. First, we need to understand that "culture" today is a source of capital. What is at stake then is simply the racist appropriation of the productive energies of minorities (young, racialized, precarious) equivalent to the sexist appropriation of matrimonial work in the social domain: invisibilized labor. This is what Brian Massumi refers to when he writes that "even those in the 'under-class' are 'productive workers' to the extent that they invent new styles that are commodified with lightning speed for 'cross-over' audiences" (1993, 16).

The second process occurs in the heterotopic experience of popular culture by the middle-class consumer. Like the nineteenth-century bourgeois who wandered in low-income neighborhoods for the thrill, his contemporary bro visits the ghetto by going on YouTube and is the one who buys gangsta rap albums in retail stores. This is also why misogynistic rap is still successful in these days of political correctness. Far from evidencing a constituent trait of popular street culture, it is mostly the reflection of the libidinal drives of those who consume these types of products, for a large part, privileged and confused teenagers. Indeed, they have to deal with the conflict that emerges between their heteronormative desires, shaped largely by a visual culture characterized by a hyper-sexualization of femininity unilaterally centered on the masculine gaze, and the official discourse of gender equality favored by their own social class. What they can find in the heterotopia provided by this simulacrum of a popular sexist culture, capitalized by the music industry, is a temporary relief from their mental struggle to juggle between the two, a place to cultivate their sexist fantasies while still being socialized in a class culture infused with mainstream feminism.

Broadly speaking, it is through a similar mechanism that the cultural industry reproduces the society desired by the state while giving itself airs of transgression or even of dissident aspirations, particularly in the elitist social circles of contemporary art and social critique. This could be why it is perfectly fine today for artists to perform a critical discourse against the state in a publicly funded institution or to give talks at Google's headquarters to denounce the so-called "attention economy." What happens then is simply the absorption of rebellious energies into the illusion of heterotopic experiences or the simulacra of social struggle for the obedient subjects of capital and the capitalist state. That way, revolutionary drives are redirected toward consumerism in the same way that my hip-hop self was spending money on "streetwear" clothes and rap CDs from multinational corporations during my rebellious teenage years.

So, you may ask, why did I share this charming story? I did so simply to emphasize that heterotopias are not fundamentally emancipatory, which is a common misreading of Foucault. Like everything, escaping psychic or libidinal repression through the creation of heterotopic spaces often leads to processes of capitalist assimilation. Transpose this logic to queerness as heterotopia to straight society. This assimilation process is much in vogue these days, evident when queer is turned into a dress code or a marketing argument. In fact, by channeling anti-normative surges into bounded, commercial spaces of sociality, heterotopias can sustain compliance to normative culture and temporalities. Take, for example, the queer, wild, druggy, and sexual parties attended on weekends so that one can live a normal life during the week. What these events tend to produce, other than their undeniable value in terms of body and pleasure politics, is the containment of minoritarian impulses into manageable settings.

The matter is somehow to flip this balance, and overcome the grip of normality over daily existence. Foucault's concept allows me to develop the communal ideal as a form of heterotopia from the logics of capital, a required "outside" to freely celebrate the value of difference, and experiment with social practices deviating from the dominant logic of individualism. In that sense, communal is a principle of persistent heterotopia with regard to capital. It is the progressive consolidation of psychosocial patterns of solidarity and extended care, through the construction of shared spaces that resist the temporalities of capital, opting instead for non-climactic and non-linear rhythms of existence. The communal is about co-making history, a collective, polyvocal laboratory that shapes the narratives of a re-sensitized future.

Locating the communal

ME O'Brien's (2019) essay *Communizing Care* recounts how self-organized operations of communality emerge to support political confrontation with the state or capital. Notably, O'Brien mentions the direct-action protest camps of Standing Rock in the Dakotas, the Zone à Défendre (ZAD) phenomenon in France, or the squares movements in Greece. In these instances of prolonged insurgency, people often develop practices for collectively procuring food, cooking, and shared eating; for sleeping arrangements in proximity to each other; for sharing child-rearing responsibilities; and aiding disabled comrades. Even if these sites of protest are not exempt from acts of misogyny, homophobia, and sexual violence, O'Brien insists that their collective and political character provides a better forum to contest and challenge such dynamics than the isolated family. They see it as a privileged laboratory for the collectivization of reproductive labor. Indeed, in opposition to the commodified care practices governed by the capitalist economy, what these practices reveal is a potential space of non-alienating interdependence.

Even though the following parts of their essay consist of speculative narratives of revolutionary communist insurrection, they raise a relevant concern for the establishment of a communal space of event, which is necessary for social heterogeneity, an inevitable requirement to avoid falling into the dangers of parochialism. This is where the queer element comes in, in its valuing of the preciosity of difference. This is also the reason why they are right in writing that "queer culture, queer leadership, and queer movements are an essential resource to communist struggles pursuing richer forms of human freedom."

I will now expand on two ideal-types of queer communal spaces, which I selected because they present the potential, but also reveal the complexity, of a queer communal kinship, or the exercise of social reproduction for non-normative subjectivities under capitalism. While these spaces combine the first two aspects of the traditional family model, namely a living arrangement and an affective constellation, they generally lack the third, which is transmission and filiation. The whole question, then, is to study the factors that restrict that possibility in order to develop a sustainable force of resistance from within our patriarcho-capitalist society.

In that sense, I'm interested in the intersection between queer gender politics separate from the heteronormative family and non-capitalist event spaces which are by necessity surrounded and partly impregnated by capitalist logics and subjectivities. There lie the concrete utopias of queer communal kinship. These points of intersection are inevitably actualized in precarious, ambiguous, and porous formations. Nonetheless, since we are reaching here a point of potential praxis, I draw on two concrete examples, that is, the queer shared household and the queer militant squat.

The Queer Shared Household

In her essay *The Ties That Bind, the Family You Find, Or: Why I Hate Babies,* Kai Cheng Thom (2019) describes her feeling when, in her mid-twenties, the atmosphere of radical queer kinship surrounding her crumbled in favor of a large return to normativity, noticing her friends' embrace of monogamy and middle-class codes of domesticity. This acceleration of micropolitical capitulation is a phenomenon I personally observed in straight circles as well, at the same period of life; an erosion of criticality with regard to the type of lifestyle pursued by previous generations.

This normative process is synchronous with the arrival of babies, as if parenthood systematically sealed the end of the lived practice of radical politics. It is true that for queers, it usually implies a difficult process of compliance to normative standards in order to attain legal or economic access to the possibility of parenthood. Social reproduction is a touchy topic for queer communities. For a social group whose bodies and right to reproduction are always called into question, childbirth and child-rearing take on an especially deep significance (103).

In US queer culture, the notion of "chosen family" is often summoned to describe social formations that take over the role of support and care normally sustained by the biological family, giving instead a sense of close community to otherwise stigmatized individuals. Kath Weston (1997) defines chosen family as consisting of friends, partners and ex-partners, biological and non-biological children, and others who provide kinship support. This is certainly a relevant framework to locate forerunner signs of queer communal kinship.

Nonetheless, what Thom describes is a process in which these chosen families dissolve in the background when "real family," often defined as bringing children into the equation, comes in. Thom thus formulates this important question: "Is chosen family another way of saying second-best family" (105)? To put it differently, what pushes queers and non-queers alike to prioritize projected material comfort and reproductive self-accomplishment through normative assimilation over political engagement and social bonds that exist outside of the privatized cocoon of the couple? What strategies could help in counterbalancing this tendency?

There seem to be two potential resolutions to this issue. The first is to push for an amelioration of the material conditions of non-normative lives, a very tricky question for sure. That may partially involve a "queering" of architecture and urbanism, which to a large extent would consist of combined dynamics of collectivization and singularization. There is a direct causal link between standardizing living infrastructures and sustaining heteronormativity, and experiments on the infrastructural level seem like the only way out. The second is to push for a cultural symbolic order that values difference and experimentation along, and not against, normative conformism and stability, something that would require, among other things, the denaturalization of the normative, essentialist family. But not only.

There seems to be one social phenomenon that moves along these types of considerations for our study, which is the increasing reliance of young people on the practice of home-sharing or households consisting of biologically and sometimes affectively unrelated individuals living in self-contained houses and apartments. Shared living arrangements, by no means a new phenomenon, are becoming more widespread for a number of reasons: an increasing mobility required to secure employment, the rise of a precarious class with limited access to ownership, and the erosion of middle-class security and conservative family values that previously saw people marry, secure housing, and get children at an early age.

Home-sharing in urban centers can be seen as a form of adaptation in the shell of the old, with single-family houses occupied by heterogeneous groups of individuals who repurpose the present architecture for different modes of living. This is one factor explaining why cohabitation is often seen as inferior to the standard of individual housing, with promiscuity issues resulting from unadapted spatial arrangements. The other main factor is symbolic. To a large extent, home-sharing is still perceived as something linked with youth, a temporary phase until one reaches the financial independence to access private housing, with notions of privacy and autonomy symbolically affiliated with adulthood.

What I will focus on here is nonetheless a very specific phenomenon, which is the emergence of middle-class young adults from European capitals who are suspicious of normative adulthood, and, as a consequence, develop flexible, non-standardized responses to work and domesticity (Heath 2004, 162). This phenomenon, when it stabilizes in shared living arrangements, provides a privileged terrain for the development of a communal ethic. Diverging from the constant propertarian and individualist mindset dominating a capitalist existence, collective living provides the singular experience of an extension of communal practices. Spaces, activities, food, clothes, tools, supplies, but also psychological and emotional support, are then potentially turned into shared experiences and resources.

Additionally, this way of living, organizing daily life, and negotiating domestic relationality defies norms linked to the role of the family in the social organization and opens a heterotopic communal space in a social landscape dominated by middle-class familialist ideology. In this context, "close platonic friendships such as those that exist within some shared households have the potential to present a challenge to normative expectations of household formation based on the conventional heterosexual couple" (Heath 2004, 175), as in developing lasting intimate bonds, especially in "more-than-two" formations, outside of the couple-form or the biogenetic family.

There is also an effect linked to the scale of these social formations. In my youth, I had the chance to live in houses where we were sometimes more than eight or ten roommates living together, with people regularly coming and going. This created an oscillation or blurring between a sense of kinship and a sense of community, which is precisely the type of open, semi-stable affective formation that I seek for queer communal kinship. These spaces are also places to organize events, parties, and exhibitions experimenting outside the normalizing supervision of the state as it is operated in cultural institutions, another way to blur the border between domestic and public space with generative effects of communality.

More specifically, the emergence of queer shared households, or shared living arrangements where domestic groupings collectively identify as "queer," is an exciting phenomenon. These households provide potential safe spaces for queer experimentation and healing toward a re-valuation of difference. My experience of living in such places has shown me repeatedly how the concrete, daily negotiation of collectively sharing a queer home constitutes a most precious laboratory of social rituals by negotiating routines beyond stable identities, normative projections, and binary gender norms. Furthermore, these spaces also provide a uniquely benevolent context to alleviate gender-related traumas, notably in terms of (re)building body- and sex-positivity. Of course, a more in-depth study would dive further into the psychosocial specificities of queer shared households. For now, I simply advocate for their engaged pursuit, since I could clearly locate there what I would qualify as early signs of queer communal kinship.

However, it is important to mention a major limitation of home-sharing in terms of stability. Most often, these living arrangements depend on landlords whose decisions depend, in turn, on financial considerations that challenge the safe consolidation of these household formations. This is also one of the reasons why non-normative communities often move to peri-urban and rural areas, thereby losing some of their visibility and potential influence over the mainstream. To my experience, these islands of communality explode when people are kicked out, and, more often than not, these moments of dissolution mark the time in which many choose to retreat in normative households.

This issue needs to be addressed specifically in relation to the question of social reproduction since some level of stability is required to raise children in satisfactory conditions. Publicly owned infrastructure supporting this type of living arrangements might help. Furthermore, without going as far as advocating for the seizure of assets, since that will probably never happen under our current political regimes, a responsible reaction in line with socialist ethics would be to put in place measures going against the financialization of real estate; for example, by discouraging the use of real estate as financial assets with a heavy taxation on the rental market, or a rigid regulation on speculative practices to push prices as low as possible. This may be naive speculation, but it appears to me that only by imposing legal conditions under which there would be no interest in owning more real estate than is necessary for living we could approach material conditions supporting the ideal, enshrined in the *Universal Declaration of Human Rights* (UN General Assembly, 1948), that housing is a right. Therefore, I like to repeat this as much as possible: *real estate speculation should be a crime.*

Such measures would help in resisting the capitalist assimilation of queer social tendencies, the commodification of communal impulses at stake behind the phenomenon of what is currently signified through the term "co-living" (Coldwell 2019). What hides behind this commercial lingo is the trending mobilization of venture capital and start-up culture on the commodification of housing practices required by the living conditions of the new precariat class, a normalizing bulldozer annihilating all potential of disruptive communal living in the city. Indeed, it is very easy to see how these initiatives are deeply ingrained with heteronormative, conservative bourgeois ideology, since it is both where the capital comes from and culturally constituent of the middle-class people designing these housing "products." At the extreme, "co-living" infrastructures display bold aspects of classist insensitivity, visible in absolutely indecent exploitative instances such as the "pod living" phenomenon in some major American cities. Facing this new tendency, there may only be one more radical field of action to undertake, even though it brings some more issues to the table: squatting.

The Queer Activist Squat

Activist squats occupy a unique position in the urban social landscape, because they give visibility to what is usually hidden, that is, anti-normative postures and radical politics applied in the concrete experience of living in the city. Generally speaking, squats are illustrative of micropolitical tragedies, as the symptom of politics of exclusion. Next to homelessness, squatting is part of the "constitutive outside," the unavoidable residue from the community of integrated urban citizens. Therefore, militant squats are not to be idealized as radical spaces of inclusion. More often than not, squatting empowers those who are not completely helpless, those who already know a bit "how to do it" from their prior socialization (Matthey 2009).

Nonetheless, squatting is a direct action aimed at fulfilling a collective need through social disobedience against the oppressive sacralization of property rights, with housing increasingly treated as commodity instead of social good. As such, it is a grassroots political intervention at the core of urban politics (Martínez 2013, 6). The richness of that sociological terrain is that it mobilizes individuals who are generally more radicalized in their anti-normative aspirations and in their questioning of capitalist logics as, indeed, squatting defies in its very principle that of inegalitarian private property. Facing the violence of neoliberal subjectivity, which generalizes a mercantile sensibility in our lived modalities of relation, the activist squat is a shelter that protects from the accusing or scornful gaze of the integrated city dweller and corresponds to an ideal of living-together carrying alternative values to the dominant ones (Aguilera 2011, 1–2). Most importantly, activist squats develop social practices following logics that are antithetical to capital, because they inscribe human activity into cooperative and non-wage social relations, for example, by producing meals, baking bread, or organizing various events, such as concerts, parties, workshops, children's activities, and so on. In the city, militant squats are some of the rare spaces providing non-commercial alimentation, entertainment, and education, reaching diverse populations by their direct implantation into sometimes stigmatized neighborhoods. Nonetheless, they often face stigma and distrust themselves because they can also be sources of real and fantasized nuisances for their surrounding populations, when they are not simply seen as dangerous parasites. Their non-normativity and lack of allegiance to capital can, to a large part, explain their otherness. In terms of symbolic territoriality, and beyond its dimension of civil disobedience, squatting is arguably the only pure form of non-capitalist claim over the city.

Indeed, squatting is almost systematically vilified by mainstream media, with the repeated televisual dumping of sensationalist depictions in which brave landlord–citizens are dispossessed from their hard-won properties by racialized gangsters, or privileged bourgeois artists are shown as parasitizing fancy locations for their own fantasies. In terms of legislation, the tendency is to increase repression, not tolerance. In different countries around Europe, squats gets evicted on a daily basis, with criminal convictions becoming commonplace. Of course, capital has also put its grip on the phenomenon of vacant buildings: in the Netherlands *antikraak* is to squatting what co-living is to home-sharing, undermining tenants' rights and exploiting their precarity (Buchholz 2012); in France the phenomenon of "tiers-lieux" (Besson 2018) wraps a sometimes commercial or financial reterritorialization of temporary occupations into narratives of collectivity and experimentation (Deloménie 2021), driven by hip, bourgeois urbanites.

Fundamentally, squatting, as a grassroots practice, touches on an affective attachment to the urban living condition in which many of us have been growing, or the "right to the city" as conceptualized by Henri Lefebvre (1968) in his eponymous work. In recent years, the concept has been reclaimed by social movements and thinkers as a call to action to reclaim the city as a co-created space, defending the exercise of a collective power to reshape processes of urbanization (Harvey 2008), understood as the right to experience the joy of a concentration of difference(s), the stimulation provided by a swarm of human creativity, or the poetics of the city. This seems like a reasonable reaction to the grim reality in urban centers that turn more and more into bland commercial deserts or touristic theme parks, where everything is expected, calculated, and normalized under the rule of finance capital. In this dynamic, squats don't occupy a neutral position, as they are often implicated in complex processes of gentrification.

In the past few years in European capitals, there has been an emergence of "queer" self-identified activist squats, assuming forms of queer activism in their local activity, intervening in a subcultural landscape clouded by a nimbus of masculinity and often implicitly understood as a male-connoted terrain (Doucette and Huber 2008). In this context, autonomous queer spaces provide a radical platform to explore and extend a number of practices and strategies that first emerged in the late 1970s as a way of making visible new forms of resistance against patriarchal power structures, endemic sexual violence, and other shared forms of oppression (Amantine 2011, as cited in Vasudevan 2015, 178). For a moving account of these dynamics from the 1970s movements of gay liberation, one could not avoid the delightful example of the *Brixton Gay Community* in London (Cook 2013; TahaFHassan 2014), with its territory of ten squatted houses sharing a communal "fairyland" made by smashing the dividing garden walls (Bettocchi 2021, 76), a concrete utopian space which, according to the nostalgia-filled accounts of its members, could never have existed without the possibilities offered by the practice of squatting.

To take a more recent example, we could mention the squat Liebig 34 in Berlin, an initiative self-defined as a "queer anarcho-feminist house project" (Azozomox 2014, 191). This is an exemplary case of QCK prefigurative politics, as Alexander Vasudevan (2015) relates in his extensive study of Berlin's squatting scene:

"as a queer space, the residents of Liebig 34 have self-consciously attempted to forge a prefigurative geography that anticipates a collective form-of-life whilst disrupting the traditional family structure" (178). Here we have the case of a social experiment with the denaturalization of the traditional family model formally inscribed into its agenda.

In my experience, traveling across European cities, queer occupations are spaces of flourishing imagination, small ecosystems of *enthusiasm-in-difference* conveniently dropped in the middle of uniforming depression-suffocating cityscapes. Anyone who participated in queer squat events will surely agree that behind the difficulties and tensions produced by precarious life conditions and systemic violence, these are social laboratories sustaining joyful energies of experimentation, something that any healthy society should dearly cherish. These are privileged spaces to deploy modes of interaction and social rituals that defy patriarcho-capitalist relational logics. A growing body of work (Oblak and Pan 2019; Cook 2013; Vanelslander 2007) is starting to identify the types of social and discursive practices emerging from these concrete and symbolic spaces. It also points at the inherent difficulties in concretizing queer politics in long-term, fixed spaces in which people try to share a political project and daily life at the same time (Vanelslander 2007, 10).

Institutionalized squats, occupied public buildings transformed into community centers, are another specific type of squatting agency. These enact, to a certain extent, a celebration of difference with situated sociocultural practices that don't fit into a specific institutional mold such as those (the museum, the theater, the library) most often made innocuous because everything happening there is predetermined, safe, and easy to swallow. Going against the norm of cultural institutions poisoned by political sanitization, quantitative logics, and economic imperatives, these are blurring the borders between legal and illegal, public and private, institutional and autonomous. Is this not a tiny bit queer?

Of course, it is important not to downplay the hard reality of squatting, which restricts its potential for strategies of QCK.

Squatting frequently involves harsh and stressful conditions of living in suboptimal housing conditions, in coexistence with a large range of psychosocial issues produced by the city, and recurrent harassment by authorities. Similar to home-sharing, squatting is often perceived by its practitioners as a temporary, transitory practice before acceding to "proper" housing. In his review of the European squatting scene, Miguel A. Martínez (2013) notices that "[r]adical squatters do not always expect to squat during the entirety of their lives; this is, in fact, very unlikely […]. For most people who squat for living, squatting is a stage along the way to a permanent residence" (13).

Finally, it is important to stay conscious of the social reality of the field in order to discern what falls under the concern of social struggle, so that squatting does not become the exclusive practice of the few, co-opted by political discourses of inclusivity and turning into enclaves of privileged individuals engaging in romantic processes of self-precarization. This is an especially sensitive matter, with activists rightfully emphasizing the importance of consolidating support between different branches of the squatting movement. As a Dutch collective recently involved in occupation actions recalls us: "We want housing for all, not just for a select group of 'artists and freethinkers'" (Anarcha-Feminist Group Amsterdam 2021).

"The anticapitalist struggle is an intersectional one. Liebig34 provides a perfect example. In their fight against housing being a commodity, capitalism, and patriarchy, they have been a symbol for radical queer feminism" (Freedom News 2020). In the squat scene more than anywhere else, all good things come to an end. The spectacular eviction of Liebig 34 on October 9, 2020, involving a heavy armored car and an acrobatic break-in by police forces in riot gear, ended thirty years of occupation. What the tragically voyeuristic police-guided tours given to the press after the eviction (BILD 2020; Ruptly 2020) reveal is the harsh living conditions of activists who sacrificed material comfort to maintain a life in accordance with their ethics and the obscene lack of public support for an institution that has fiercely carried its radical values over three decades of neoliberal social decrepitude.

Theory and Practice

In her essay *Theory's Method? Ethnography and Critical Theory,* Marianna Poyares (2021) poses a fundamental concern regarding the actualization of research: "How to select which social struggles to focus upon, in a world of total administration and totalizing domination" (361). This is the ethical question that led me into developing this conceptual assemblage of QCK, as a tool to distinguish in the complex constellation of my social surroundings which parts were worth further investigation, in a combined objective of activism, research, and inter-subjective development. This raises the question of the place theory can occupy in daily existence, as a privileged framework to assist the making of decisions in personal and collective life events. The widespread exercise of critical theory is paramount to this decision-making.

What I have seen lacking in virtually every socializing institution I traversed — family, school, workspace, and, to a certain extent, cultural and artistic institutions — is the practice of theory as a self-reflexive, interdisciplinary, transformative, and materialist tool to grasp critically the stakes of the world surrounding us. In this regard, education is key. Critical skills should be cultivated and valued as early as primary school and continuous education pursued throughout adulthood. Furthermore, I would not only encourage the consumption but the production of critical theory, especially in a form of political auto-ethnography in order to shape ethics and praxis. In that sense, collective practices of reflection and articulation of thought should also be encouraged. There is no other way out from the toxic individualism that permeates our cultural era, and the democratization of critical thinking should be our main concern in the struggle against the instrumentalization of desire for the interests of capital. As Braidotti (2008) elegantly puts it, "critical theory is about strategies of affirmation. Political subjectivity or agency therefore consists of multiple micro-political practices of daily activism or interventions in and on the world we inhabit for ourselves and for future generations" (16).

It is largely through books that my emancipatory drives began to materialize into concrete realizations because I have been fortunate enough to come across some important works that opened my capacity for critical thinking. Even so, this has been a tedious and highly contingent process, which could have been initiated much earlier and developed much more efficiently if incentives to take part in critical thought existed in our mainstream socio-cultural landscape. It is a shame that this is not a more accompanied and encouraged practice in our supposedly civilized but highly dysfunctional culture.

Theory is useful, in that it helps us locate our points of struggle and shape our political strategies. Regarding the two ideal types of queer communal spaces I previously developed, for example, it appears that landlord lobbying groups and financial capital have political decision-making in a tight grip, something which, by the way, would be seen as corruption under actual democratic regimes. Since these agencies enforce heteronormativity in the infrastructure of the city itself, this is a simple but illustrative case in which critical social theory helps in identifying the power structures constraining the emancipation of queer energies, since these lobbies are probably as bad, if not worse, than more obvious opponents such as the catholic church or your local homophobic politician.

The communal element is probably the most challenging in my conceptual construction, because it necessarily diverges from the topic of denaturalizing the family toward imagining a different social order. Therefore, this has only been a set of meditations on what would definitely require further research. It also served me as a guide in engaging targeted ethnographic fieldwork. I hope it can motivate some of my readers to follow similar directions. In the process of making this book, I found out that this was the most difficult chapter to write, and I can only explain that by the fact that communal is so alien to a capitalist existence.

Therefore, my communal concept is maybe a shy exposure to communism, a remixed version adapted for twenty-first-century deployment in which the communist project will have to come packaged in a refreshed format capable of infiltrating the ranks of capitalist subjectivities. One thing is for sure, nowadays in the west it is pretty much accepted to call oneself anticapitalist, but much less communist or socialist. What I know as well is that after sharing this book's manuscript with a few close friends, some of them went as far as calling me a marxist, something which never happened to me before. Just in the same way as with "queer," this interpellation actually led me into an active process of investigating that question — to be or not to be marxist? — triggering both my becoming-marxist and critical regard to concepts I had blindly taken as common sense. What this sudden realization revealed is the impact of marxist heritage throughout my autodidact philosophical formation, but also the importance of disseminating our ideas through identificatory priming. I guess the cover of this book unveils my complete lack of formal subtlety for that matter.

3. kinship

If communal was about imagining a non-capitalist family, kinship is about a non-essentialist one. Kinship, in its simplest understanding, is a way of ordering relationships. Loaded with its history in modern colonial epistemology, the term will nonetheless be appropriated by feminist anthropologists to designate forms of relationships that are binding or even constitutive but that exceed the particular form of the family. In that perspective, family can be seen as simply one historical instance of kinship, and kinship theory as a body of knowledge that emerges from attempts to abstract the governing principles of relational practices of intimacy observed in a given culture (Freeman 2008, 295).

This allows kinship theory to be used as a conceptual framework for the denaturalization of intergenerational ties by highlighting the constructivist nature of blood metaphysics in our social reproduction system, and the sacralization of biogenetic reproduction in the patriarchal symbolic order. Again, while it is important to assess critically its colonial and modern heritage as a western epistemological paradigm, "kinship" is a fruitful analytical tool to assess that any relationship constituted in terms of procreation, filiation, or descent can also be made post-natally or performatively by culturally appropriate action (Sahlins 2011, 3). Thus, the study of kinship consists of asking simple questions unconditioned by our specific cultural perspective: how are basic relations of intimacy and needs organized through time and space? What are their variations and possibilities?

We can also summon kinship as a term that signifies a conscious coalition centered on relations of care and attention. This is, for example, the case with the phenomenon of "chosen families," or affinity-based families, as kinship formations generally structured around shared affections and worldviews. This is compelling because it constitutes an alternative to the imposed, inherently violent, conventional family that universalizes a specific social hierarchy among individuals. Note as well that this epistemological framework also helps us blur the border between the two traditionally separated realms of family and community, since extended kin networks can also be conceptualized in ways that go way beyond the type of structure usually associated with the concept of family.

In fact, that is the ultimate idea behind this notion of kinship and the reason for its popularity in the feminist sphere of social critical discourse, notably due to the contribution of Donna Haraway with her slogan *Make kins not babies!* (2016b, 18): the fact that all earthlings are kin, in-relation, in the deepest sense. Kinship then is only a matter of organizing the relational assemblages that populate the earth, without segregating us between species, genders, races, or generations. For a post-family agenda, "making kin" means to put forth something deeper than entities tied by ancestry or genealogy and proceed in such a way by bonding in accordance to ethical considerations. Kinship is a call to make our structures of care and attention ethically accountable.

What kinship reveals then is the inadequacy of the family as a concept for the development of ethical relational practices, particularly as regards the stakes of biological and social reproduction, unless we decided to indulge in sheer and blind primitivism. Therefore I suggest to use kinship as a tool for the denaturalization of human reproduction as it is currently dominated by oedipal narratives of biological evidence and "natural" simplifications.

Nature and Kinship

There is nothing "natural" about the way we humans live nowadays. Actually, when we think of anything "natural" in regard to humanity, we unconsciously project a primitive stage of our species in terms of technology; sticks and rocks instead of central heating and laptops. That is why we associate reproduction with something natural. Basically, we assume that the way we make babies is more or less the same as how prehistoric people did. But this obfuscates the fact that our whole existence is completely different from that of prehistoric times. Putting a dick in a vagina from which a baby rolls out is a really reductive way of understanding how emerging as a human happens in our society.

Of course, it is true that our biology restricts the range of relational possibilities for our species (Fracchia 2005, 45), and any radical feminist would be ill-advised in refuting that complex reality. Largely, however, it is our technology that defines and poses limits to the plasticity of our social connections. More importantly, in most cases, it seems irrelevant to even try to distinguish them both, as much as they are entangled into the same network of materialization and signification. This is especially the case regarding human reproduction, as much as it is mired in military–industrial histories of power relations and patriarcho-capitalist narratives, fictions of the self that inscribe human existence in rigid frameworks of restricted determinations ("it's a boy/girl!") and tragically reductive interpellations into capitalist flows of desire ("I want a baby!").

Therefore, what we need is an analytical tool that helps us avoid the deterministic and reductionist consequences of confusing abstractions such as "family" or "blood lineage" with reality, imposing them as an a priori recipe or schema on real bodies in their concrete cultural specificity. As an open theoretical tool to analyze and develop new fields of relationality, kinship relates to what John McMurtry conceptualizes as "projective consciousness" or "the ability to raise a structure in imagination and then erect it in social reality" (1978, as cited in Fracchia 2005, 44), thus making it an abstraction that is methodologically valuable for both critical and prefigurative politics.

Furthermore, against the discourses of modernity serving us with a "cheap" nature (Patel and Moore 2018) ready to be commodified for the stakes of humanity, with the rhetorical separation of nature and culture supporting extractivist narratives of ontological vulgarity, kinship maintains the focus on our ecological interdependency that we need to adequately address in our planetary condition by organizing our flows of desire in sensitive or ethical ways. This is what a posthuman or non-anthropocentric kinship entails, providing us with a critical framework to deconstruct naturalized relations in western thought and hopefully bringing "nature" back from its modern status as inanimate background or consumable material, to what it really is: natureculture, our field of relationality. In that sense, kinship transcends the modern distinction of objects and subjects, as identification between kins can be porous and multi-level. By being kin with another human, I might also desire to be kin with the microbes, bacteria, and other entities that are fluidly constituent of this particular body.

Queer Kinship

Queer kinship has been studied extensively over the last decades. However, this has in most cases consisted of sociological studies of LGBT parenting that do not integrate the philosophical and utopian dimensions of queerness into their considerations. This is where the essay of Laura Heston, *Utopian Kinship?*

The Possibilities of Queer Parenting, comes handy. Indeed, as it is concerned with queer futurity, Heston's work aims to find out how inside queer families children can become vehicles for imagining new familial relations and ways of being. Therefore, her research corresponds to how kinship intervenes in my conceptual articulation, following that question: "what is the place for reproductive relations within imaginative queer world-making projects" (2013, 246)?

For sure, the scope of her research is rather limited: twenty interviews conducted in the region of Massachusetts in the United States. Although she avows herself that "no families [she] met were perfect models of problem-free, antinormative, queer kinship" (253), the report she makes from her fieldwork allows me to distinguish three characteristic traits of a queer kinship:

- **Criticality**: queerness as a politicized identity leads to approaching parenthood and childrearing with a knowledge and application of queer politics. For example, parenting formations that eliminate the need for heterosexual sex, and, therefore, heterosexuality as a fundamental of reproduction, can be performed as a political act.

- **Complexity**: stepping out from the model of the biological nuclear family engages in the necessary embrace of more complex familial constellations. Chosen parenting also faces the additional complication of negotiating with legal frameworks that only legitimate conventional families, sometimes requiring a certain dose of creativity. She illustrates this fact with the example of a couple that decided to marry for the sole goal of having the trans man who gave birth to their child inscribed as the father on the birth certificate, through a tricky legal maneuver that would not have been possible without their marriage.

- **Fluidity**: the LGBTQ parents with an investment in alternative family forms she interviewed had fluid and open ideas about who is or could be part of their families. This shapes a concept of family as inclusive, expansive, and ever-evolving rather than biologically exclusive and static. In this case, the meaning of the word "family" gets close to the anthropological notion of kinship as a contingently determined social formation.

What her work points at is the emergence of "real," publicly assumed queer kinship formations that completely dismiss the need for any sort of reference to the heterosexual dyad nor to biological reproduction. If for most of them, the people in her study identify with the social roles of "fathers" and "mothers," this is due to their personal identification with one side of a binary spectrum of gender and not due to some essentialist necessity. Ultimately, these traditional roles are rendered obsolete by a truly queer framework of parenting. This should be distinguished from queer families that model themselves on the heterosexual ideal of family, most famously like the example of the drag houses depicted in the film *Paris Is Burning* (Livingston 1991), even though they compose an implicit critique of the frequent lack of affection in this normative cultural model. Additionally, it is of course possible for "straight" families to engage in queer parenting practices or construct non-normative families. I'm only pointing to an idealized notion of queer kinship detached from the heteronormative patterns that structure our society.

Indeed, deconstructing traditional gender roles in the family and with them, gender normativity as a whole, is the key aspect of a kinship formation invested in the project of queer worldmaking, which is to invite children to interact with the expanded field of possibilities offered by breaking with the gender binary, which otherwise constitutes the default, presumably natural terrain in which most children and their bodies automatically locate themselves (Ward 2013, 243). The benefit of queer kinship is to avoid the limiting and often violent effects of that naturalized order and lies in the discovery of new forms of relating in collectivities that are non-oedipal and non-biological. It allows us to escape the bourgeois family values that prescribe a naturalized set of priorities, such as children's wellbeing over friendship or political engagement. That is a trap that can only lead to serving children with an impoverished relational landscape mired into the grim state of capitalist realism (Fisher 2009).

Queer kinship also provides a framework to imagine a counterculture to the hegemonic heteronormative script of life, for which making children is seen as the ultimate achievement and in which childbearing often results in a disengagement from radical politics. Instead, it is a matter of integrating the raising of children as integral to a social praxis in which the psychic realm of desire for reproduction and the material realm of establishing or consolidating a counterpublic are conceived as entangled aspects of the same political project. This demands breaking from normative generationality and detaching from the metaphysical notion of lineage, where children are necessary agents in our experimental landscape of world-making practices, not extensions of our egos.

Moreover, articulating a project antinomic to the cult of the family, supporting a concern for redistributive justice, requires the realization of what we might have to let go. Most evidently, the question of inheritance, as an indisputable factor in the maintenance of economic inequality in our society, has to be put up for discussion. This could be the main site of resistance, as it also constitutes the most evident resource for redistribution. I only emphasize the need to push for this conversation in order to shake up our cultural views on this issue, and ultimately campaign for the transformation of our legal frameworks. In this context, cultural actors speaking out in favor of full or partial abolition can be a valuable strategy to bring publicity to the topic.

I conceive of kinship as a trigger for the imagination, an invitation to contemplate, individually and collectively, the shapes that our future social formations might take. Imagining what sorts of bonds we would like to experiment with in non-patriarchal, denaturalized, sensitive, and ethical approaches is the self-reflexive process needed to avoid repeating the mistakes perpetuated by the internalized model of "the family." In that sense, the simple semantic gesture of swapping family for kinship in these interrogations already allows one to proceed in such an exercise with a slightly expanded freedom of thought.

A Materialist Relational Framework

In opposition to the essentialist qualities associated with the imaginary of the family, kinship relies on a materialist understanding of the socio-discursive mechanisms and patterns that shape the organization and distribution of practices of care and attention. We are far past the time of drawing circles and triangles on whiteboards, and kinship is to be conceived as the study of a complex entanglement of forces sustaining life in specific cultural formations. To come back to the ballroom "houses" of *Paris Is Burning*, as the classic and most commented instance of QCK, what these historical examples hint at us by their sole name, is the importance of that concrete, physical space. Beyond the heavy symbolic charge associated with the word "house" for young queers of color often left without one after having been chased from their previous homes, these alternative kinship formations are actualized through and determined by their physical implantation in the geography of the city as safe territories sheltered from the gaze of the heteronormative society (Rio 2020, 131), but dependent on their interactions with such social order to secure its material conditions of sustenance.

Indeed, QCK is not something that will pop out of nowhere. As we have seen earlier through the evocation of two potential sites of emergence, the shared household and the activist squat, QCK requires the creative and opportunistic distortions of existing architectural space — as Anna Lowenhaupt Tsing (2015) famously put it, we need to learn how to live on the ruins of (patriarchal) capital. Increasingly marginalized squatting and assimilated communal living won't make it for QCK to flourish perennially, and strategies attentive to the material conditions of QCK-leaning groups must be combined with initiatives of anti-assimilationist queerchitecture. In that regard, favoring access to property might ironically reveal itself central, since anti-normative queers are not traditionally versed in capital accumulation but still need a place to live, ideally one that does not participate in their systemic exploitation.

To secure housing independence strategically relieves one from economic subordination to the normative order. In that sense it seems important to emphasize the co-constitution of the spatial and the political. Promising initiatives are emerging, notably with the model of "Community Land Trust" which enables emancipation from rental feudalism while resisting the commodification of real estate in the city. In fact, this appears as the most direct approach to resist the speculators' takeover and maintain the right to the city for queer formations by taking urban land permanently out of the private market. Unfortunately, these initiatives are often modeling their real estate developments on the needs of the nuclear family. Furthermore, they only constitute a minor, but in a sense prefigurative, set of engagements in the struggle for housing, which is not likely to overtake the increasingly aggressive privatization of that basic human need. There is an everlasting need for more political action on that matter, as it is central to the organization of sociality and political imagination beyond capital. To quote a slightly misplaced but appropriately emphatic Malcolm X: "Revolution is based on land. Land is the basis of all independence. Land is the basis of freedom, justice, and equality" (1963).

Again, I am sort of stepping outside my topic. Indeed, though neither an architect nor an urban planner, I might still formulate the challenge: how to strive for difference when authoritative standardization is the norm? Metaphorically, how do you deal with aspirations and drives for funny shapes when everything has to fit in perfect squares? Pragmatically, what do you think has factored in defining this book's format? Modularization and economy of means are two concerns that are often hard to combine. Nonetheless, we should aim for that.

What is important to cover is what limits the formation of kinship in the queer and communal terrains, where presence is generally contingent and offers no real equivalent to the traditional family in terms of support and security. In many cases, squatters and cohabitants still conceive family relationships based on the bourgeois heteronormative model, which may have been altered to varying degrees but whose broad outlines are nonetheless preserved. Moreover, these substitutes to the family home generally melt away at the time of displacement toward couple stability and dyadic dwelling, reinforcing the erosion of communal practices in the forging of embryonic nuclear families. Since the ethics of kinship I propose are intrinsically connected to communal modes of organizing, it matters to consider the material implications of developing home-sharing as a long-term collective engagement instead of a temporary dwelling practice for adolescence, and queer communal parenting as an affirmative praxis instead of a disparaging alternative to the couple lifestyle.

There is another important aspect of kinship that I would like to address, namely that there is no fundamental reason to constrain our cultural imagination to homebound kinship models. In fact, that would be inheriting a limiting constraint from a conservative familialist framework of thought. Quite the opposite. It is precisely where architectural or other spatial regulations of sociality limit the range of experimentation for kinship formations, that people get creative outside and around these constraints, notably through technological usages that alleviate distances or improve remote communication. Therefore, I again advocate for fluid physical borders of kinship, ones that break away from the private space of family, which strategically resonates with the whole history of feminism.

Kinship as Narrative

After treating the topic of inheritance, I diverted to the issue of housing to indicate where and how our current kinship formations lead to inegalitarian social conditions, and what a critical materialist angle can provide in conceiving alternative kinship formations. What else is constitutive of our kinship model? One evident pillar of that naturalized order seems to be the stability of names, and by extension identity. Performatively speaking, it is a bit of a concern that most of us still rely on our patriarchal names for our daily operations. Letting this go might be part of the cure to the patriarchal obsession with post-mortem longevity.

What I am touching upon here is the question of kinship as a bonding story, or narrative of belonging, and what this produces in the material constitution of sociality. Let's take the example of religion. What leads people to religions isn't simply reason, but far more importantly: emotion, habit, fear, and tradition. People stick with their religious beliefs because they like the rituals, the communal meals, the yearly traditions, the beautiful architecture, the music, and the lovely stories read out in the buildings of their cults. Similarly, we stick to the family because we like the rituals (the stability of our individual roles in the household, the yearly traditions), the narratives (belonging through the bloodline, genetic transmission), and the reassurance in finding adequate socio-material conditions for our well-being (tailored state institutions and public infrastructure) if we maintain our allegiance to that model.

Against the dogmatic effects of such hegemony, there is the need to develop alternative narratives of belonging, emancipated from essentialist accounts that narrow major aspects of social reproduction within the realm of dyadic parental units, such as the previously cited "family of choice" or Foucault's "friendship as a way of life" (Foucault 2000, 135). What kinship is about is the definition of organizational principles or narratives for our material practices of social reproduction along ethical or egalitarian principles. The design of such narratives, motivated by the concern of manufacturing human beings, not in the most efficient but in the most sensitive way, requires full-on pragmatics exempted from romantic pollution, or residues from our bio-primitive conception of childbirth and care. In that sense, kinship is a call to address the intolerable conditions of the present: the ways reproductive labor is still largely unequally distributed among society, making it the everlasting cause of intersectional feminism; the ways state-incentivized family structures still or even increasingly produce and sustain socioeconomic inequalities; and the ways in which our complacency with a non-critical scrutiny of normative family ties still supports violent and asymmetrical power relations between men and women, parents and children, adults and elders.

One way to articulate that complex issue is by trying to find what concrete answers can be given to Mitchell Cowen Verter's call: "Can we not embrace a non-patriarchal vision of the home as a site for the enactment of responsibility for the needs of ourselves and other people, a place for caring, refuge and hospitality: a model for empathetic sociality" (2013, 6)? How to get there? Better than our dear Haraway's butterfly stories, Sophie Lewis's advocacy for a distributed procreation and a denaturalized gestation strikes me as a good starting point: "We need ways of counteracting the exclusivity and supremacy of 'biological' parents in children's lives; experiments in communizing family-support infrastructures; lifestyles that discourage competitiveness and multiply nongenetic investments in the well-being of generations" (2019, 100).

Even so, I would not risk myself in making too much of a statement here. This is not a book about queer parenting, as my dialogue with practitioners of such endeavors struck me as underlining the complexity inherent in practicing parenthood in a non- or anti-normative fashion. More research has to be done. The communal children from the 1970s and '80s gay liberation have now reached adulthood, and there is certainly much to learn from their experience with the critical distance that is now in reach. In parallel, researchers are exploring how the privileged terrain of LGBTQ families reveals children's ability, thus potential agency, in (re)defining their kinship bonds (Dyer, Sinclair-Palm, and Yeo 2020). In both cases, we need to understand how oppressive structures can be challenged by positive, generative, and prefigurative measures and strategies, while scrutinizing such counter-practices with great and critical care. This is a project of emancipation through knowledge.

4. A Joyful Synthesis

As we are getting close to an end, it might be time to elucidate how this whole story inscribes itself in the feminist legacy, specifically in relation to its new materialist strand. For this, I rely on an opportune optical metaphor, namely diffraction. In contemporary feminist theory, diffraction is often employed figuratively to denote a more critical and difference-attentive mode of consciousness and thought (Geerts and van der Tuin 2016). In that sense, diffraction is to be contrasted with "reflexivity" as the traditional way of producing knowledge. For example, for Haraway, diffraction is about making "a difference in the world" by paying attention to "the interference patterns on the recording films of our lives and bodies" (Haraway 1997, 16). As an invitation for my readers, I would like to gently point at Barad's (2007) quantum elaboration on that idea, as definitely one of the tastiest piece of intellectual cake I have relished in recent feminist philosophy.

In the meantime, what does this idea bring in for a study such as the one I attempted in this book with the family? In answering this question as well as making a little joke regarding our common christian cultural background, I point to a specific aspect of their conceptual systems that resonates with my own, that is, the trinity structure. Indeed, similarly to Barad's quantum journey into the epistemo-onto-ethical, and Haraway's lively elaboration on sym-bio-genesis (to which I could add, in a similar vein, Guattari's trio of ecologies), my system of QCK emerges as a sort of holy trinity, attempting an anarcho-communo-feminist diffractive maelstrom.

What these conceptual frameworks have in common is the concern for accountability, for "putting everything on the table" in order to assess, evaluate, transform, and rethink our patterns of relationality. This is what Haraway's "staying with the trouble" (in the mud of continuously asymmetrical power relations), Barad's "agential realism" (the entanglement of ontological, epistemological, and ethical concerns), as well as Stengers's "cosmopolitical proposal" (grossly, politics as ethoecological assemblage), and finally QCK are all about, which is to define egalitarian frameworks to think or rethink the social. In Stengers's words, "equality does not mean that [the protagonists] all have the same say in the matter, but that they all have to be present in the mode that makes the decision as difficult as possible, that precludes any short-cut or simplification, any differentiation a priori between that which counts and that which does not" (2005, 1003).

Within such a concern for social analysis, thinking diffractively implies a self-accountable, critical, and responsible engagement with the world. In making-world together, there is no space for instrumentalizing strategies or privileged, traditionally masculinist postures of refusal or autonomy. Accountability means first and foremost an ethical self-involvement in the practice of social and institutional transformation. This is why Barad's quantum relational ontology or Law's (2019) material semiotics are so appealing to new materialist and posthumanist scholars: because they tackle individualism at its core, revealing that difference is an ontological issue and cannot just be a political demand.

Non-normative Temporalities

QCK is a denaturalized space of sociality exempted from the exclusionary and hierarchalizing imperatives of a structuring biogenetic reproduction. It therefore asks what kinds of interage, instead of inter-generational, bonds can be shaped when we exclude from the equation the familialist temporalities of succession and inheritance. This raises the question of the potential temporalities of QCK, a timespace in which the rhythm of generations would be rendered obsolete, seen as pure anachronism to be left behind with the possessive and hierarchical framework of the traditional family.

This resonates with what Halberstam has called a middle-class logic of reproductive temporality (2005, 4), or the fact that in western cultures, we suppose longevity as the most desirable future and pathologize modes of living that show little or no respect for it. In his book *In a Queer Time and Place,* Halberstam indeed elaborates on what shapes the temporality of normative western subjectivity, characterized by the valorization of long periods of stability. He specifically expands on the rhythms of reproduction which were traditionally ruled by strict bourgeois rules of respectability and scheduling for married couples. In that sense, "family time" refers to a normative daily life schedule — early to bed, early to rise — that accompanies the practice of child-rearing, a timetable governed by an imagined set of children's needs. It also refers to the temporality of inheritance which structures the ways in which values, wealth, goods, and morals are passed through family ties from one generation to the next, a temporality that is attuned to the logic of capital accumulation.

Once again it might be relevant to point at the cultural role of psychoanalysis in this bourgeois normative scheme, as a framework that reinforces the conventional narratives and institutions of romance, establishing dramas of love, sexuality, and reproduction as the dramas central to living, and installing the normative institutions of intimacy, mainly the couple and the intergenerational family, as the proper sites for providing the life plot in which a subject has "a life" and a future (Berlant 2012, 86). In contrast, Halberstam exposes the sort of temporalities that qualify the life of queer subjects, speculatively associating with this label the whole range of individuals who, by their distanciation from normative reproductive and familial time, live to a certain extent outside the logic of capital accumulation: ravers, club kids, HIV-positive barebackers, rent boys, sex workers, homeless people, drug dealers, and the unemployed; those who live outside "the organizations of time and space that have been established for the purposes of protecting the rich few from everyone else" (Halberstam 2005, 10).

Note here that I only refer to queer temporalities and am not really touching on communal or kinship. The point is that for long, these components of my conceptual ensemble have not really co-existed in any legible sense. Queerness was associated with precarious and non-sustaining forms of kinship, while communal living was restricted to counter-publics, thus happening outside the scope of mainstream legibility. Both were considered marginal practices, either temporary as youthful escapades quickly caught up by the inexorable grip of society, or in the worst case leading to social exclusion or death. What happens when queerness ceases to be the characteristic of a marginal subject position and infuses its discourses into mainstream culture? When communal living is democratized as a legitimate urban lifestyle, as an alternative to the nuclear family dwelling instead of simply a buffer between teenage and adulthood or a countercultural fantasy?

As queer representation flourishes in the media, arguably in highly normalized fashion, many artists and theorists today, be they indulging in heteronormativity for their private or domestic life, seem to joyfully engage with queer discourse in their professional practices. Cultural and commercial institutions alike are raising liberal feminism as a new secular religion, even if largely ornamental to a capitalist lifestyle and inscribed in a distribution of subjectivity-shaping narratives — alongside neo-fascism and evo-psy masculinism — facilitated by the digitalization of sociality into echo chambers and niche markets. At the same time, young and less young people are seduced or pushed into practices of communal dwelling to sustain their presence in the city. In that whole confusing landscape, the old homosexist term "breeders," mocking the straights for their bland lifestyle of biological reproduction, seems to lose its contemporary relevance. Queer parenting, as an increasing phenomenon, challenges the notion that queerness and normative temporalities of child-raising are necessarily distant to each other.

To be clear, I don't aim to turn queers into breeders (how evil would that be!) nor to celebrate communal living as a normalized adaptation to the neoliberal flexibility and precarization of the workforce. Rather, my goal is to affirm that queers can enjoy babies too, something that was much less facilitated a few decades ago, and current socio-economic conditions might to a certain extent encourage more complex queer, and communal, kinship normative formations to emerge. Observed through a critical lens, this combination of recent developments might raise virtual potential for spreading anti- and non-capitalist approaches toward the social, if one is prompted with the sort of ethics that could drive future QCK formations in their inscription in the temporal fabric of society.

As much as kinship formations based on biogenetic reproduction are here to stay, at least for a bit, we are not safe from an upsurge of (hetero)normative violence considering the current political climate, and it would be highly delusional to consider the emergence of half-decent queer representation in mainstream media as a secure victory over the dominant obscurantism with regard to sexual minorities. As I previously developed with the necessity of post-gender safe spaces of expression, we need similarly performative theoretical discourses at the level of our arrogant ambitions, even though that should not refrain us in parallel from aiming for a certain realism in our assessments of the social.

The spatiality of Difference

Beyond temporality, the challenge also lies in the spatial organization of sociality and its progressive hypernormalization (Curtis 2016). What we see happening with the process of heavy urban gentrification and corporately mediated online filter bubbles is the erosion of inter-class mixing, the process through which a society can allow its members to realize and problematize the tensions inherent to the complexities of their social field.

Samuel R. Delany, in his study of the epuration of Times Square in the name of "family values and safety," is right to see lurking behind this flag of familialist values "a wholly provincial and absolutely small-town terror of cross-class contact" (Delany 1999, 153), as a retrograde move in relation to the development of emancipated forms of civic subjectivity offered by contemporary megacities. Again, the queer has to be erased from the map for the reason that it resists capitalist assimilation. Indeed, the queer culture of public sex created spaces for interclass encounters, a richness of interaction unconstrained by the framework of a commercial transaction. Referring to this context, Delany theorizes what he calls "contact relations," a mode of interaction that took place in a non-capitalist space of event that is vanishing today. This reduction of sociability to acts of capitalist exchange produced by the organized gentrification of previously free zones of interaction is exemplified by the "quality of life campaign" carried in New York by its mayor Rudy Giuliani in the 1990s (Vitale 2008). The sexually driven sociability generative of cultural intermingling and collective belonging has been replaced by fragmented and capitalized modes of interaction based on the exploitation of individual desires.

Beyond the fact that this erasure of queer practices and subsequent normalization has been justified throughout the last decades by moral principles affiliated with the cultural norm of the family, I return to the tension behind understanding kinship and community as two separated realms. The fact that we mostly live in urban, complex, multicultural communities requires a healthy dose of class and cultural mixing, so that the "other" can be understood and welcomed as neighbor, coworker, sharer of the same space. In order to be kin, one must be able to intimately relate to the other. For the first case, the matter is sharing; for the second, caring. The aim of a reflection around the concept of communal kinship is to render this distinction fluid, supported by the intervention of queer as the anti-normative, generative force of inclusion.

Communities, like kinship formations, are imaginary institutions made of affects and desires (Anderson 1983). However, they generally don't serve the same social function. The first is about evolving together in the same spatial arrangement in heterogeneity but with minimal tension and resentment; the second is about providing a privileged frame of care and attention, a concrete togetherness in intimacy that safely complements the generative social realm of community, necessarily more abstract considering its scale. Note that my intention is not to renaturalize kinship as the exclusive location of care in my speculative construction. "How can we take care of each other?" is a question that must be addressed at the level of the communal, where complexity is intrinsically shaped by our planetary condition. Nonetheless, theorizing this distinctive sphere of intimacy and belonging might be required in the process of generalizing a relational regime of care beyond the privatized paradigm of the family.

It would be delusional or dangerously totalizing to require all community members to care for each other at the level of kins. This is why enclaved intentional communities are irrelevant to my interest, since they neglect the multiculturalism that fundamentally characterizes our global, interconnected natureculture. On the contrary, they conform and isolate their communities, while mostly maintaining kinship structures of possessive and exclusive filiation present. To my understanding, any ambitious shift in desire politics cannot decently be expected to emerge in a paranoid state of retreat. I advocate the fluidity, the opening toward the other that is at stake in queer social formations, the becoming-kin of communal companions, the becoming-communal (acceptance of otherness) of kins. Only with these mingled dynamics may we achieve a cohesive social order that does not overly prioritize kins or rigidly exclude parts of its community.

5. conclusion

Queer is about desire (not only sexuality): the force of *becoming-other*. *Communal* is about practice (not only theory), about doing: the performative machine of our conceptual apparatus, the potency to iterate change. *Kinship* is the process of iteration itself: the focus of an extended political project that takes over the family institution and counteracts the limited scope of short-termist political formations. Queer is utopian, communal is prefigurative, and kinship is (re)productive. Queer should be used as a mindset, communal as a method, and kinship as a focus. Queer opens (difference), communal generates (pragmatism), kinship activates (imagination). Taken together as a conceptual melting pot producing a synthetical sensibility, QCK is an affinity — one could say a "structure of feeling" — for non-referential performative acts of association driven by an ethical sensitivity.

I hope this chapter has inspired you to consider the emancipatory and critical potential that lies in the imaginative combination, or critical entanglement, of these three concepts I developed. The aim of my enterprise, driven by the importance of reshaping or reinventing the family institution, is to nourish this conversation. I am thus not trying to formulate a concrete proposal, but only point at leads and clues that can be found in social and discursive practices developing across our cultural landscape. *Queer communal kinship now!*

A RELATIONAL SHIFT

Emancipatory politics must always destroy the appearance of a
"natural order," must reveal what is presented as necessary and
inevitable to be a mere contingency, just as it must make what
was previously deemed to be impossible seem attainable.

— Fisher (2009, 17)

To denaturalize the family is an ambitious project. My hope
here is that I managed to articulate a concise argumentation and
gather accessible concepts that can be useful in operating a shift
in the ways we think about our social relations, especially those
of major importance in our lives: relations of intimacy, proximity, and care. For this matter, rebuilding communality, empathy,
and compassion is a huge task to pursue on the psychosocial
ruins left by our history of patriarchal capitalism or capitalist
patriarchy. These two words are essentially describing the same
thing, an inextricably entangled formation through which the
family institution naturalizes private property and normalizes
exclusion, accumulation, and hierarchization.

The western family today is the crystallization of colonial,
patriarchal, and capitalist logics, cognitive and relational habits
that every informed individual today should attempt to purge
from their own social practices as their own ethical responsi-

bility. In that sense, putting oneself in a couple molded on the heteronormative model, settling down in a single-family home, and producing children today, if this is indeed the most privileged social posture rewarded for one's docility and complacency with these rotten, absolutely rotten and rotting values, is surely not the best thing to do, for it is to submit to the airs of the past one's own desires, locked in a truly terrifying and suffocating historical impasse.

Nonetheless, "the family" occupies such a prominent place in our public discourses and symbolic orders that rejecting it outright might be counterproductive for groups aiming to challenge the hierarchies and psychosocial patterns that drive our natureculture evolution. On the contrary, any conscientious and structured political collective must integrate in its considerations the matter of social reproduction as it is occurring among its own ranks. Still, in any case, the denaturalization of the bourgeois heteronormative model appears to be imperative. The family structure we have upheld as the cultural ideal for the past decades has been a catastrophe for many. More than ever, it is time to figure out better ways to grow, live, and die together.

Beyond the problematized denaturalization of the family, I have sought to expose and develop three concepts that, from my situated perspective, seem of the highest relevance to our political challenges: *queer* as a considerably powerful force of transformation that should not be neglected by the political leaders and thinkers of the left; *communal* as an identified set of psychosocial practices and tendencies to be nourished and cherished in the context of a capitalist existence; and finally, *kinship* as a determined realm of sociomaterial relations that must go through a necessary rethinking for us to develop a more ethical culture in the west.

We must elevate our standards of sensitivity, care, and attention if we want a more just and perennial society to emerge. The family, as the abstraction used to describe where we live together and relate intimately and intergenerationally is a privileged terrain to work in that direction. The depatriarchalization of our culture is a necessary step in the imagination of a non-capitalist future, and we won't get there if we stick with our current family model. We must leave the comfort of our collective habits and find out other ways to relate. What power can we reclaim when we stop artificially producing scarcity in our social lives (RAD Unconference 2019, 27)?

We all grew up in a world that cultivates values of individualism, competition, domination, and accumulation. These principles are deeply ingrained in us and prevail in most of our thoughts, actions, and political decisions. As much as we must fight for policy changes and denounce the oppressive power structures in place, we must also struggle to transform ourselves and our own cognitive processes, even if that represents a considerably difficult challenge. To be clear, I do not want to designate the individual as the unit of social transformation, but rather to insist on the interdependently embodied materiality of the struggle for emancipation, in order to establish psychosocial change as a communal and exhilarating journey. I am convinced in the necessity to engage collectively with changing the narratives that frame our existences. We need to start writing and disseminating different stories of the social or, better, stories of *difference*.

In the words of a much-regretted British theorist: "The libidinal attractions of consumer capitalism [need] to be met with a counterlibido, not simply an anti-libidinal dampening" (Fisher 2012, 134). For one regime of desire to succeed in replacing another, it must have sufficiently strong properties of attraction. QCK is the call for such an enterprise, for the development of bonding patterns and affective sequences that escape the capitalist logics inscribed in our relational practices, supported to a large extent by our normative habits and drives with their tint of familialist ideology. One last time, I would like to emphasize the joyful enthusiasm to be found in the practice of denaturalizing the family and imagining its future, considering the body of literature available and the amount of collective energy gathering around these issues today. Such a wonderful time! How could there be challenges more exciting than reinventing family and home for the post-capitalist society, more stimulating than discerning what in our political assessments still falls under the blinding veil of bourgeois ideology?

Note that these pages do not explicitly tackle the intersectional, postcolonial, postsecular, or posthumanist dimensions which, among others, would add precious subtlety to these questions. Moreover, to write about the family without seriously diving into its contemporary entanglements with labor or technology cannot but result in a limited and limiting account, while putting aside a more traditional focus of feminist and queer theory on sexuality and embodiment remains a difficult and still unsatisfactory decision. As a piece of utopian, subjective literature or "low theory," the scope of this book is thus by its very nature limited in its purview.

Nevertheless, this is a matter of priority. Mine is the critical study and development of alternative affects and modes of living that attempt to thrive both in integration to the urban social fabric and beyond the repetition of normative social relations. In doing so, we begin to redefine the city as a field of openness. This is partly why I have not wanted to dive too much into concrete examples of QCK practices, so as not to condition the reader in approaching it in an overly predetermined manner. On the contrary, by simply evoking terrains or fields of potential emergence, I try to focus our attention on the possibilities and limitations that emerge from existing material conditions, the basis of which we should develop our reflections and experiments. It is also in an effort at brevity that I have allowed myself this exercise in abstraction, as simply one movement in an open-ended story.

REFERENCES

Adorno, Theodor W. 1974. *Minima Moralia: Reflections from Damaged Life.* Translated by E.F.N. Jephcott. London: New Left Books.

Aguilar, Jade. 2013. "Situational Sexual Behaviors: The Ideological Work of Moving toward Polyamory in Communal Living Groups." *Journal of Contemporary Ethnography* 42, no. 1: 104–29. DOI: 10.1177/0891241612464886.

Aguilera, Thomas. 2011. "Les squats, entre contestation et résistance." *Métropolitiques.eu,* April 1–4. https://metropolitiques.eu/Les-squats-entre-contestation-et.html.

Anarcha-Feminist Group Amsterdam. 2021. "Action Report: Anarcha-feminist Squatting during 8th of March in Amsterdam." *Green Anti-Capitalist Media,* March 10. https://greenanticapitalist.org/feminist-squat-amsterdam-8m/.

Anderson, Benedict R. O'G. 1983. *Imagined Communities: Reflections on the Origin and Spread of Nationalism.* London: Verso.

Azozomox. 2014. "Squatting and Diversity: Gender and Patriarchy: In Berlin, Madrid and Barcelona." In *The Squatters' Movement in Europe: Commons and Autonomy* as *Alternatives to Capitalism,* edited by Claudio Cattaneo and Miguel A. Martínez, 189–210. London: Pluto Press. DOI: /10.2307/j.ctt183p1wf.

Badinter, Élisabeth. 2001. *L'amour en plus: Histoire de l'amour maternel (XVIIe–XXe siècle).* Paris: Flammarion.

Bammer, Angelika. 2015. *Partial Visions: Feminism and Utopianism in the 1970s.* Oxford: Peter Lang.

Barad, Karen. 2007. *Meeting the Universe Halfway: Quantum Physics and the Entanglement of Matter and Meaning.* Durham: Duke University Press.

Barbetta, Pietro, Maria Esther Cavagnis, and Inga-Britt Krause. 2022. *Ethical and Aesthetic Explorations of Systemic Practice: New Critical Reflections.* New York: Routledge.

Barrett, Michèle, and Mary McIntosh. 2015. *The Anti-Social Family.* London: Verso.

Berger, Brigitte, and Peter L. Berger. 1983. *The War over the Family: Capturing the Middle Ground.* Garden City: Anchor Press/Doubleday.

Berlant, Lauren. 2011. *Cruel Optimism.* Durham: Duke University Press.

———. 2012. *Desire/Love.* Earth: punctum books.

Berlant, Lauren, and Michael Warner. 1995. "Guest Column: What Does Queer Theory Teach Us about 'X'?" *Publications of the Modern Language Association of America* 110, no. 3: 343–49. DOI: 10.1632/S003081290005937X.

Bessière, Céline, and Sibylle Gollac. 2020. *Le genre du capital: Comment la famille reproduit les inégalités.* Paris: La Découverte.

Besson, Raphaël. 2018. "Les tiers-lieux culturels: Chronique d'un échec annoncé." *L'observatoire* 52 (January): 17–21. DOI: 10.3917/lobs.052.0017.

Bettocchi, Milo. 2021. "Fairies, Feminists and Queer Anarchists: Geographies of Squatting in Brixton, South London." PhD Thesis, University of Nottingham.

BILD. 2020. "'Liebig 34' in Berlin: So sieht es in dem geräumten Haus aus." *YouTube,* October 8. https://www.youtube.com/watch?v=ST8PVzfZNAU.

Blaylock, Reed. 2020. "For Linguists, It Was the Decade of the Pronoun." *The Conversation,* January 8. http://theconversation.com/for-linguists-it-was-the-decade-of-the-pronoun-128606.

Bloch, Ernst. 2016. *Du rêve à l'utopie: Entretiens philosophiques.* Edited by Arno Munster. Paris: Hermann.

Boggs, Carl. 1978. "Marxism, Prefigurative Communism, and the Problem of Workers' Control." *Radical America* 11, no. 6 (Winter): 99–122. https://theanarchistlibrary.org/library/carl-boggs-marxism-prefigurative-communism-and-the-problem-of-workers-control/bbselect.

Boutang, Pierre-André, Gilles Deleuze, Claire Parnet. 2004. *L'abécédaire de Gilles Deleuze avec Claire Parnet.* Edited and translated by Charles J. Stilvale. Paris: Editions Montparnasse.

Braidotti, Rosi. 2006. *Transpositions: On Nomadic Ethics.* Malden: Polity Press.

———. 2008. "In Spite of the Times: The Postsecular Turn in Feminism." *Theory, Culture & Society* 25, no. 6: 1–24. DOI: 10.1177/0263276408095542.

Braidotti, Rosi, and Rick Dolphijn. 2014. "Deleuze's Philosophy and the Art of Life, or: What Does Pussy Riot Know?" In *This Deleuzian Century: Art, Activism, Life,* edited by Rosi Bradotti and Rick Dolphijn, 13–36. Leiden: Brill. DOI: 10.1163/9789401211987.

Buchholz, Tino, dir. 2012. *Creativity and the Capitalist City.* TUNi Productions. https://vimeo.com/49254956.

Burgett, Bruce, and Glenn Hendler, eds. 2020. *Keywords for American Cultural Studies.* 3rd edition. New York: NYU Press.

Butler, Judith. 2011. *Bodies That Matter: On the Discursive Limits of "Sex."* Abingdon: Routledge.

Cacioppo, John T. 2008. *Loneliness: Human Nature and the Need for Social Connection.* New York: Norton.

Campbell, Andrew M. 2020. "An Increasing Risk of Family Violence during the Covid-19 Pandemic: Strengthening Community Collaborations to Save Lives." *Forensic Science International: Reports* 2. DOI: 10.1016/j.fsir.2020.100089.

Christophers, Brett. 2020. *Rentier Capitalism: Who Owns the Economy, and Who Pays for It?* London: Verso Books.

Cohen, Jeffrey Jerome. 2012. "Monster Culture (Seven Theses) (Extract)." In *Speaking of Monsters,* edited by Caroline Joan S. Picart and John Edgar Browning, 15–18. New York: Palgrave Macmillan. DOI: 10.1057/9781137101495_2.

Cohn, Jesse. 2010. "Sex and the Anarchist Unconscious: A Brief History." *Sexualities* 13, no. 4: 413–31. DOI: 10.1177/1363460710370649.

Coldwell, Will. 2019. "Co-Living: The End of Urban Loneliness — or Cynical Corporate Dorms?" *The Guardian,* September 3. http://www.theguardian.com/cities/2019/sep/03/co-living-the-end-of-urban-loneliness-or-cynical-corporate-dormitories.

Collins, Patricia Hill. 1998. "It's All in the Family: Intersections of Gender, Race, and Nation." *Hypatia* 13, no. 3 (Summer): 62–82. DOI: 10.1111/j.1527-2001.1998.tb01370.x.

Cook, Matt. 2013. "'Gay Times': Identity, Locality, Memory, and the Brixton Squats in 1970's London." *Twentieth Century British History* 24, no. 1 (March): 84–109. DOI: 10.1093/tcbh/hwr053.

Cowen Verter, Mitchell. 2013. "Undoing Patriarchy, Subverting Politics: Anarchism as a Practice of Care." In *The Anarchist Turn.* London: Pluto Press. https://theanarchistlibrary.org/library/mitchell-cowen-verter-undoing-patriarchy-subverting-politics-anarchism-as-a-practice-of-care.

Creamer, Anita. 2011. "The Widowhood Effect: A Spouse Dies, Then Soon, Another." *The Seattle Times,* February 7. https://www.seattletimes.com/seattle-news/health/the-widowhood-effect-a-spouse-dies-then-soon-another/.

Cryle, Peter, and Elizabeth Stephens. 2017. *Normality: A Critical Genealogy*. Chicago: University of Chicago Press.

Curtis, Adam, dir. 2016. *HyperNormalisation*. BBC.

David, Gaby, and Carolina Cambre. 2016. "Screened Intimacies: Tinder and the Swipe Logic." *Social Media + Society* 2, no. 2. DOI: 10.1177/2056305116641976.

Day, Richard J.F. 2011. "Hegemony, Affinity and the Newest Social Movements: At the End of the 00s." In *Post-anarchism: A Reader*, edited by Duane Rousselle and Süreyyya Evren, 95–116. London: Pluto Press. DOI: 10.2307/j.ctt183pb1v.

Dean, Jodi. 2019. *Comrade: An Essay on Political Belonging*. London: Verso.

de Boever, Arne, and Warren Neidich, eds. 2013. *The Psychopathologies of Cognitive Capitalism: Part One*. Berlin: Archive Books.

de Castro, Julio Cesar Lemes. 2014. "O Amor Virtual Como Instância de Empreendedorismo e de Reificação." *Galáxia* 14, no. 27 (June): 72–84. DOI: 10.1590/1982-25542014115069.

Dejeans, Louise. 2017. "L'opposition au mariage pour tous en France: Entre retour du religieux et laïcisation de la religion." *Interrogations* 25 (December). http://www.revue-interrogations.org/L-opposition-au-Mariage-pour-tous.

Delany, Samuel R. 1999. *Times Square Red, Times Square Blue*. New York: New York University Press.

de las Heras Gómez, Roma. 2019. "Thinking Relationship Anarchy from a Queer Feminist Approach." *Sociological Research Online* 24, no. 4: 644–60. DOI: 10.1177/1360780418811965.

Deleuze, Gilles. 1994. *Difference and Repetition*. Translated by Paul Patton. New York: Columbia University Press.

Deleuze, Gilles, and Félix Guattari. 1972. *L'anti-Œdipe: Capitalisme et schizophrénie*. Paris: Les Éditions de minuit.

———. 2009. *Anti-Oedipus: Capitalism and Schizophrenia*. New York: Penguin Books.

Deloménie, Alexandre. 2021. "Wonderland: La merveilleuse illustration de la fracture sociale à Paris." *Le Club de*

Mediapart, July 11. https://blogs.mediapart.fr/alexandre-delomenie/blog/110721/wonderland-la-merveilleuse-illustration-de-la-fracture-sociale-paris.

Demarinis, Susie. 2020. "Loneliness at Epidemic Levels in America." *EXPLORE* 16, no. 5 (September–October): 278–79. DOI: 10.1016/j.explore.2020.06.008.

Doucette, Erika, and Marty Huber. 2008. "Queer-Feminist Occupations." *Transversal,* June. https://transversal.at/transversal/0508/huber-doucette/en.

Duggan, Lisa. 1993. "The Trials of Alice Mitchell: Sensationalism, Sexology, and the Lesbian Subject in Turn-of-the-Century America." *Signs* 18, no. 4 (Summer): 791–814. https://www.jstor.org/stable/3174907.

———. 2004. *The Twilight of Equality? Neoliberalism, Cultural Politics, and the Attack on Democracy.* Boston: Beacon Press.

Duncombe, Jean, and Dennis Marsden. 1993. "Love and Intimacy: The Gender Division of Emotion and 'Emotion Work': A Neglected Aspect of Sociological Discussion of Heterosexual Relationships." *Sociology* 27, no. 2: 221–41. DOI: 10.1177/0038038593027002003.

Dustan, Guillaume. 2021. *The Works of Guillaume Dustan,* Vol. 1: *Novels.* Translated by Daniel Maroun. Los Angeles: Semiotext(e).

Dyer, Hannah, Julia Sinclair-Palm, and Miranda Yeo. 2020. "Drawing Queer and Trans Kinship with Children: Affect, Cohabitation, and Reciprocal Care." *Review of Education, Pedagogy, and Cultural Studies* 42, no. 4: 257–76. DOI: 10.1080/10714413.2020.1724764.

Esquivel-Santoveña, Esteban Eugenio, Teri L. Lambert, and John Hamel. 2013. "Partner Abuse Worldwide." *Partner Abuse* 4, no. 1: 6–75. DOI: 10.1891/1946-6560.4.1.6.

Evans, Julian. 2016. "The Experiment of Friendship: Anarchist Affinity in the Wake of Michel Foucault." MA Thesis, Concordia University. https://dspace.library.uvic.ca//handle/1828/7226.

Fahs, Breanne. 2010. "Radical Refusals: On the Anarchist Politics of Women Choosing Asexuality." *Sexualities* 13, no. 4: 445–61. DOI: 10.1177/1363460710370650.

Fassin, Éric. 2009. "Entre famille et nation: La filiation naturalisée." *Droit et société* 2, no. 72: 373–82. DOI: 10.3917/drs.072.0373.

———. 2015a. "Mobilizing Publics: Intellectuals, Activists, and the Political Work of Representation." 3rd International Conference of the Group for Social Engagement Studies, Center for Advanced Studies in Southeastern Europe, University of Rijeka, Belgrade, Serbia, November 21.

———. 2015b. "Ni tout à fait la même, ni tout à fait une autre: Du PaCS au 'mariage pour tous.'" 6th AFS Congress, University of Versailles Saint-Quentin-en-Yvelines, Guyancourt, France, July 2. https://www.canal-u.tv/chaines/afs/vers-une-denaturalisation-du-genre-de-la-sexualite-et-de-la-famille-semi-pleniere-avec.

Fine, Agnès, and Agnès Martial. 2010. "Vers une naturalisation de la filiation?" *Geneses* 1, no. 78: 121–34. DOI: 10.3917/gen.078.0121.

Firestone, Shulamith. 1970. *The Dialectic of Sex: The Case for Feminist Revolution.* New York: Morrow.

Fisher, Mark. 2009. *Capitalist Realism: Is There No Alternative?* Winchester: Zero Books.

———. 2012. "Post-capitalist Desire." In *What We Are Fighting For: A Radical Collective Manifesto,* edited by Federico Campagna and Emanuele Campiglio, 131–38. London: Pluto Books.

Floyd, Kevin. 2009. *The Reification of Desire: Toward a Queer Marxism.* Minneapolis: University of Minnesota Press.

Fortino, Sabine. 1997. "De filles en mères: La seconde vague du féminisme et la maternité." *Femmes, Genres, Histoire* 1, no. 5: 1–17. DOI: 10.4000/clio.421.

Foucault, Michel. 1980. *Power/Knowledge: Selected Interviews and Other Writings, 1972–1977.* Edited by Colin Gordon. New York: Pantheon Books.

————. 1984. "Des espaces autres: hétérotopies." *Foucault. info.* https://foucault.info/documents/heterotopia/foucault. heteroTopia.fr/.

————. 1994. *Dits et écrits: 1954–1988.* Edited by Daniel Defert, François Ewald, and Jacques Lagrange. Paris: Gallimard.

————. 2000. *Essential Works of Foucault 1954–1984,* Vol. 1: *Ethics: Subjectivity and Truth.* Edited by Paul Rabinow. Translated by Robert J. Hurley. New York: The New Press.

Fracchia, Joseph. 2005. "Beyond the Human-Nature Debate: Human Corporeal Organisation as the 'First Fact' of Historical Materialism." *Historical Materialism* 13, no. 1: 33–62. DOI: 10.1163/1569206053620915.

Franke, Katherine. 2013. "Becoming a Citizen: Reconstruction Era Regulation of African American Marriages." *Yale Journal of Law & the Humanities* 11, no. 2: 251–309. https://digitalcommons.law.yale.edu/yjlh/vol11/iss2/2.

Freedom News. 2020. "Interview with Liebig34 Squat in Berlin as It Resists Eviction." *Freedom News,* September 26. https://freedomnews.org.uk/interview-with-liebig34-squat-in-berlin-as-it-resists-eviction/.

Freeman, Elizabeth. 2008. "Queer Belongings: Kinship Theory and Queer Theory." In *A Companion to Lesbian, Gay, Bisexual, Transgender, and Queer Studies,* edited by George E. Haggerty and Molly McGarry, 293–314. Oxford: Blackwell Publishing. DOI: 10.1002/9780470690864.ch15.

Frémeaux, Isabelle, and John Jordan. 2012. *Les sentiers de l'utopie.* Paris: La Découverte.

Fromm, Erich. 1955. *The Sane Society.* New York: Rinehart & Company, Inc.

Gapova, Elena. 2016. "Gender Equality vs. Difference and What Post-socialism Can Teach Us." *Women's Studies International Forum* 59 (November–December): 9–16. DOI: 10.1016/j. wsif.2016.09.001.

Garhan, Amy. 2013. "Couple Privilege: Having It Doesn't Necessarily Make You an Asshole (But It Might)." *Solo Poly,* February 5. https://solopoly.net/2013/02/05/couple-privilege-having-it-doesnt-necessarily-make-you-an-asshole-but-it-can/.

Geerts, Evelien, and Iris van der Tuin. 2016. "Diffraction & Reading Diffractively." *New Materialism,* July 27. https://newmaterialism.eu/almanac/d/diffraction.html.

Gilligan, Carol, and Naomi Snider. 2018. *Why Does Patriarchy Persist?* Malden: Polity Press.

Gilman-Opalsky, Richard. 2020. *Communism of Love: An Inquiry into the Poverty of Exchange Value.* Chico: AK Press.

Gordon, Uri. 2018. "Prefigurative Politics between Ethical Practice and Absent Promise." *Political Studies* 66, no. 2: 521–37. DOI: 10.1177/0032321717722363.

Gracia, Enrique, Christina M. Rodriguez, Manuel Martín-Fernández, and Marisol Lila. 2020. "Acceptability of Family Violence: Underlying Ties between Intimate Partner Violence and Child Abuse." *Journal of Interpersonal Violence* 35, nos. 17–18: 3217–36. DOI: 10.1177/0886260517707310.

Griffin, Jo. 2010. *The Lonely Society?* London: Mental Health Foundation.

Guattari, Félix. 2014. *The Three Ecologies.* London: Bloomsbury Academic.

Halberstam, Jack. 2005. *In a Queer Time and Place: Transgender Bodies, Subcultural Lives.* New York: New York University Press.

———. 2011. *The Queer Art of Failure.* Durham: Duke University Press.

Halliday, Roy. 1997. "Bourgeois Families in a Free Nation." *Formulations.* http://freenation.org/a/f43h1.html.

Halperin, David M. 1989. "Is There a History of Sexuality?" *History and Theory* 28, no. 3 (October): 257–74. DOI: 10.2307/2505179.

Hammack, Phillip L., David M. Frost, and Sam D. Hughes. 2019. "Queer Intimacies: A New Paradigm for the Study of Relationship Diversity." *The Journal of Sex Research* 56, nos. 4–5: 556–92. DOI: 10.1080/00224499.2018.1531281.

Haraway, Donna J. 1989. *Primate Visions: Gender, Race, and Nature in the World of Modern Science*. Abingdon: Routledge.

———. 1997. *Modest-Witness@Second-Millennium. Femaleman-Meets-Oncomouse: Feminism and Technoscience*. Abingdon: Routledge.

———. 2016a. *Manifestly Haraway*. Minneapolis: University of Minnesota Press.

———. 2016b. *Staying with the Trouble: Making Kin in the Chthulucene*. Durham: Duke University Press.

Harvey, David. 2008. "The Right to the City." *New Left Review* 53 (September–October). https://newleftreview.org/issues/ii53/articles/david-harvey-the-right-to-the-city.

Heath, Sue. 2004. "Peer-Shared Households, Quasi-communes and Neo-tribes." *Current Sociology* 52, no. 2: 161–79. DOI: 10.1177/0011392104041799.

Hede, Helena. 2017. "In Search of 'A Chosen Community': A Study on Self-Initiated Co-housing Projects in Berlin." MA Thesis. http://lup.lub.lu.se/student-papers/record/8902029.

Hering, Sabine, ed. 2009. *Social Care under State Socialism (1945–1989): Ambitions, Ambiguities, and Mismanagement*. Opladen: Verlag Barbara Budrich. DOI: 10.2307/j.ctvbkk1vp.

Hester, Helen, and Nick Srnicek. 2017. "The Crisis of Social Reproduction and the End of Work." *OpenMind BBVA*. https://www.bbvaopenmind.com/en/articles/the-crisis-of-social-reproduction-and-the-end-of-work/.

Heston, Laura V. 2013. "Utopian Kinship? The Possibilities of Queer Parenting." In *A Critical Inquiry into Queer Utopias*, edited by Angela Jones, 245–67. New York: Palgrave Macmillan. DOI: 10.1057/9781137311979_11.

Honneth, Axel. 2012. *The I in We: Studies in the Theory of Recognition*. Malden: Polity Press.

Horne, Rebecca M., and Matthew D. Johnson. 2019. "A Labor of Love? Emotion Work in Intimate Relationships." *Journal of Social and Personal Relationships* 36, no. 4: 1190–209. DOI: 10.1177/0265407518756779.

Jackson, Stevi. 2010. "Questioning the Foundations of Heterosexual Families: Firestone on Childhood, Love, and Romance." In *Further Adventures of the Dialectic of Sex: Critical Essays on Shulamith Firestone,* edited by Mandy Merck and Stella Sandford, 113–41. New York: Palgrave Macmillan. DOI: 10.1057/9780230109995_6.

Kahn, Susan Martha. 2000. *Reproducing Jews: A Cultural Account of Assisted Conception in Israel.* Durham: Duke University Press.

Klapisch-Zuber, Christiane. 2000. *L'ombre des ancêtres: Essai sur l'imaginaire Médiéval de la parenté.* Paris: Fayard.

Klein, Naomi. 2008. *The Shock Doctrine: The Rise of Disaster Capitalism.* New York: Picador.

Klesse, Christian. 2014. "Poly Economics: Capitalism, Class, and Polyamory." *International Journal of Politics, Culture, and Society* 27, no. 2: 203–20. DOI: 10.1007/s10767-013-9157-4.

Kollontai, Aleksandra Michailovna. 1984. *Communism and the Family.* London: Socialist Workers Party.

Lakner, Christoph, Nishant Yongzan, Daniel Gerszon Mahler, R. Andres Castaneda Aguilar, Haoyu Wu, and Melina Fleury. 2020. "Updated Estimates of the Impact of COVID-19 on Global Poverty: The Effect of New Data." *World Bank Blogs,* October 7. https://blogs.worldbank.org/opendata/updated-estimates-impact-covid-19-global-poverty-effect-new-data.

Larsen, Elizabeth. 1998. "Poly Sex for Beginners." *Utne,* n.d. https://www.utne.com/politics/polysexforbeginners.

Law, John. 2019. "Material Semiotics." *Heterogeneities. net,* January 30. http://heterogeneities.net/publications/Law2019MaterialSemiotics.pdf.

Lefebvre, Henri. 1968. *Le droit à la ville.* Paris: Anthropos.

Lewis, Sophie. 2019. *Full Surrogacy Now: Feminism against Family.* London: Verso.

Livingston, Jennie, dir. 1991. *Paris Is Burning.* BBC.

Love Bailey. 2018. "Savage Ranch." *Savage Ranch.* http://engineering2tors.de/wp3tor/.

Lugones, Maria. 2007. "Heterosexualism and the Colonial/
Modern Gender System." *Hypatia* 22, no. 1 (Winter):
186–209. https://www.jstor.org/stable/4640051.

Luyten, Patrick, Anthony Bateman, György Gergely, Lane
Strathearn, Mary Target, and D. Elizabeth Allison. 2010.
"Attachment and Personality Pathology." In *Psychodynamic
Psychotherapy for Personality Disorders: A Clinical
Handbook,* edited by Peter Fonagy, 37–87. Arlington:
American Psychiatric Publishing, Inc.

MacKinnon, Catharine A. 2007. *Are Women Human? And
Other International Dialogues.* Cambridge: Belknap Press.

Malcolm X. 1963. "Message to the Grass Roots." *California State
University Northridge.* https://www.csun.edu/~hcpas003/
grassroots.html.

Manning, Erin, and Brian Massumi. 2014. *Thought in the
Act: Passages in the Ecology of Experience.* Minneapolis:
University of Minnesota Press.

Martínez, Miguel A. 2013. "The Squatters' Movement in
Europe: A Durable Struggle for Social Autonomy in Urban
Politics." *Antipode* 45, no. 4 (September): 866–87. DOI:
10.1111/j.1467-8330.2012.01060.x.

Massumi, Brian, ed. 1993. *The Politics of Everyday Fear.*
Minneapolis: University of Minnesota Press.

———. 2015. *The Power at the End of the Economy.* Durham:
Duke University Press.

Matthey, Laurent. 2009. "Bouillon Fl., 2009, Les mondes du
squat: Anthropologie d'un habitat précaire." *Cybergeo,*
November 19. DOI: 10.4000/cybergeo.22773.

McHugh, Kathleen Anne. 1999. *American Domesticity: From
How-to Manual to Hollywood Melodrama.* Oxford: Oxford
University Press.

McIntosh, Mary. 2013. "Social Anxieties about Lone
Motherhood and Ideologies of the Family: Two Sides of
the Same Coin." In *Good Enough Mothering: Feminist
Perspectives on Lone Motherhood,* 156–64. Abingdon:
Routledge.

Melucci, Alberto. 1985. "The Symbolic Challenge of
   Contemporary Movements." *Social Research* 52, no. 4
   (Winter): 789–816. https://www.jstor.org/stable/40970398.

Miller, Timothy. 1999. *The 60s Communes: Hippies and Beyond.*
   Syracuse: Syracuse University Press.

Morandini, James S., Alexander Blaszczynski, and Ilan Dar-
   Nimrod. 2017. "Who Adopts Queer and Pansexual Sexual
   Identities?" *The Journal of Sex Research* 54, no. 7: 911–22.
   DOI: 10.1080/00224499.2016.1249332.

Mouffe, Chantal. 2000. "Deliberative Democracy or Agonistic
   Pluralism." *Social Research* 66, no. 3: 745–58. https://www.
   jstor.org/stable/40971349.

Moulier Boutang, Yann. 2011. *Cognitive Capitalism.* Translated
   by Ed Emery. Malden: Polity Press.

Muñoz, José Esteban. 2009. *Cruising Utopia: The Then and
   There of Queer Futurity.* New York: New York University
   Press.

Murdock, George Peter. 1949. *Social Structure.* London:
   Collier-Macmillan Ltd.

Nal, Emmanuel. 2015. "Les hétérotopies, enjeux et rôles des
   espaces autres pour l'éducation et la formation: Lieux
   collectifs et espaces personnels." *Recherches & éducations* 14
   (October): 147–61. DOI: 10.4000/rechercheseducations.2446.

Oblak, Teja, and Maja Pan. 2019. "Yearning for Space, Pleasure,
   and Knowledge: Autonomous Lesbian and Queer Feminist
   Organising in Ljubljana." In *Lesbian Activism in the (Post-)
   Yugoslav Space: Sisterhood and Unity,* edited by Bojan Bili
   and Marija Radoman, 27–59. Cham: Springer International
   Publishing. DOI: 10.1007/978-3-319-77754-2_2.

O'Brien, ME. 2019. "Communizing Care." *Pinko* 1. https://
   pinko.online/pinko-1/communizing-care.

Oswin, Natalie. 2010. "The Modern Model Family at Home in
   Singapore: A Queer Geography." *Transactions of the Institute
   of British Geographers* 35, no. 2 (April): 256–68. https://www.
   jstor.org/stable/40647323.

Patel, Raj, and Jason W. Moore. 2018. *A History of the World
   in Seven Cheap Things: A Guide to Capitalism, Nature, and*

the Future of the Planet. Berkeley: University of California Press.

Perlman, Merrill. 2019. "How the Word 'Queer' Was Adopted by the LGBTQ Community." *Columbia Journalism Review.* https://www.cjr.org/language_corner/queer.php.

Poyares, Marianna. 2021. "Theory's Method? Ethnography and Critical Theory." In *Cultural Inquiry,* edited by Bernardo Bianchi, Emilie Filion-Donato, Marlon Miguel, and Ayşe Yuva, 345–63. Berlin: ICI Berlin Press. DOI: 10.37050/ci-20_19.

Preciado, Paul B. 2013. *Testo Junkie: Sex, Drugs, and Biopolitics in the Pharmacopornographic Era.* Translated by Bruce Benderson. New York: The Feminist Press.

———. 2018. "Lettre d'un homme trans à l'ancien régime sexuel." *Libération,* January 15. https://www.liberation.fr/debats/2018/01/15/lettre-d-un-homme-trans-a-l-ancien-regime-sexuel_1622570.

RAD Unconference. 2019. "RAD 2019 Zine." https://communitiesnotcouples.com/resources.

Red May TV. 2020. "Abolish the Family! | Red May 2020." *YouTube,* May 30. https://www.youtube.com/watch?v=8nfeTeUgBZg.

Rio, Malcolm. 2020. "Architecture Is Burning: An Urbanism of Queer Kinship in Ballroom Culture." *Thresholds* 48 (April): 122–32. DOI: 10.1162/thld_a_00716.

Roseneil, Sasha, Isabel Crowhurst, Tone Hellesund, Ana Cristina Santos, and Mariya Stoilova. 2020. *The Tenacity of the Couple-Norm: Intimate Citizenship Regimes in a Changing Europe.* London: UCL Press. https://www.jstor.org/stable/10.2307/j.ctv13xpsd5.

Rosenfeld, Michael J., Reuben J. Thomas, and Sonia Hausen. 2019. "Disintermediating Your Friends: How Online Dating in the United States Displaces Other Ways of Meeting." *Proceedings of the National Academy of Sciences* 116, no. 36: 17753–58. DOI: 10.1073/pnas.1908630116.

Rothschild, Leehee. 2018. "Compulsory Monogamy and Polyamorous Existence." *Graduate Journal of Social Science* 14, no. 1 (January): 28–56.

Rousseau, Jean-Jacques. 1999. *Discourse on Political Economy and The Social Contract.* Oxford: Oxford University Press.

Rubin, Jennifer D., Amy C. Moors, Jes L. Matsick, Ali Ziegler, and Terri D. Conley. 2014. "On the Margins: Considering Diversity Among Consensually Non-monogamous Relationships." *Psychology Faculty Articles and Research.* https://digitalcommons.chapman.edu/psychology_articles/133.

Ruptly. 2020. "LIVE: A Look inside Liebig34 Squat Building in Berlin Following Eviction." *Youtube,* October 9. https://www.youtube.com/watch?v=H9FAYQVV6pg. Blocked content.

Russell, Bertrand. 1970. *Marriage and Morals.* New York: Liveright.

Sahlins, Marshall. 2011. "What Kinship Is (Part One)." *Journal of the Royal Anthropological Institute* 17, no. 1 (March): 2–19. DOI: 10.1111/j.1467-9655.2010.01666.x.

Said, Edward W. 1978. *Orientalism.* New York: Pantheon Books.

Schwarz, Stephan, and Ingrid Sabatier-Schwarz. 2017. "Self-Organised Urban Space without Profit: Four Examples in Berlin." *PlaNext* 5: 78–90. DOI: 10.24306/plnxt.2017.05.006.

Segal, Lynne. 1987. *Is the Future Female? Troubled Thoughts on Contemporary Feminism.* London: Virago Press Ltd.

Shannon, Deric, and Abbey Willis. 2010. "Theoretical Polyamory: Some Thoughts on Loving, Thinking, and Queering Anarchism." *Sexualities* 13, no. 4: 433–43. DOI: 10.1177/1363460710370655.

Shepard, Benjamin. 2010. "Bridging the Divide between Queer Theory Sage and Anarchism." *Sexualities* 13, no. 4: 511–27. DOI: 10.1177/1363460710370656.

Sherif-Trask, Bahira. 2010. *Globalization and Families: Accelerated Systemic Social Change.* Berlin: Springer.

Silverstein, S.L. 2020. "Caring against the Family: Kinship, State, and Social Reproduction." MA Thesis,

Utrecht University. https://studenttheses.uu.nl/
handle/20.500.12932/37452.

Smith, Adam. 1759. *The Theory of Moral Sentiments.* London:
A. Kincaid and J. Bell.

Smith, Daniel Scott. 1993. "The Curious History of Theorizing
about the History of the Western Nuclear Family."
Social Science History 17, no. 3 (Autumn): 325–53. DOI:
10.2307/1171429.

Snediker, Michael D. 2009. *Queer Optimism: Lyric Personhood
and Other Felicitous Persuasions.* Minneapolis: University of
Minnesota Press.

Southbank Centre. 2015. "Europe Is Kaput. Long Live Europe!
— Slavoj Žižek, Yanis Varoufakis and Julian Assange."
YouTube, November 23. https://www.youtube.com/
watch?v=yjxAArOkoAo.

Stayton, W.R. 1985. "Alternative Lifestyles: Marital Options." In
Contemporary Marriage: Special Issues in Couples Therapy,
edited by Daniel C. Goldberg, 241–60. Homewood: Dorsey
Press.

Stengers, Isabelle. 2005. "The Cosmopolitical Proposal." In
Making Things Public: Atmospheres of Democracy, edited by
Bruno Latour and Peter Weibel, 994–1003. Cambridge: MIT
Press.

Stillwagon, Ryan, and Amin Ghaziani. 2019. "Queer Pop-Ups:
A Cultural Innovation in Urban Life." *City & Community* 18,
no. 3: 874–95. DOI: 10.1111/cico.12434.

TahaFHassan. 2014. "Brixton Fairies: Made Possible by
Squatting." *YouTube,* March 21. https://www.youtube.com/
watch?v=fZxapxG_ew4.

Thom, Kai Cheng. 2019. "The Ties That Bind, the Family You
Find, Or: Why I Hate Babies." In *I Hope We Choose Love:
A Trans Girl's Notes from the End of the World,* 100–107.
Vancouver: Arsenal Pulp Press.

Trott, Carlie D. 2016. "Constructing Alternatives: Envisioning
a Critical Psychology of Prefigurative Politics." *Journal
of Social and Political Psychology* 4, no. 1: 266–85. DOI:
10.23668/PSYCHARCHIVES.1758.

Tsing, Anna Lowenhaupt. 2015. *The Mushroom at the End of the World: On the Possibility of Life in Capitalist Ruins.* Princeton: Princeton University Press. DOI: 10.1515/9781400873548.

UN General Assembly. 1948. *The Universal Declaration of Human Rights.* Paris. https://www.un.org/en/about-us/universal-declaration-of-human-rights.

Usher, Kim, Navjot Bhullar, Joanne Durkin, Naomi Gyamfi, and Debra Jackson. 2020. "Family Violence and COVID-19: Increased Vulnerability and Reduced Options for Support." *International Journal of Mental Health Nursing* 29, no. 4 (August): 549–52. DOI: 10.1111/inm.12735.

Vanelslander, B. 2007. "Long Live Temporariness: Two Queer Examples of Autonomous Spaces." *Affinities: A Journal of Radical Theory, Culture, and Action,* January 11. https://ojs.library.queensu.ca/index.php/affinities/article/view/6163.

Vasallo, Brigitte. 2017. "Pensée monogame, terreur polyamoureuse: Brigitte Vasallo." *Non monogamie féministe,* February 23. https://nonmonogamie.com/2017/02/23/pensee-monogame-terreur-polyamoureuse-brigitte-vasallo/.

Vasudevan, Alex. 2015. *Metropolitan Preoccupations: The Spatial Politics of Squatting in Berlin.* Hoboken: Wiley Blackwell.

Vitale, Alex S. 2008. *City of Disorder: How the Quality of Life Campaign Transformed New York Politics.* New York: New York University Press.

Ward, Jane. 2013. "Radical Experiments Involving Innocent Children: Locating Parenthood in Queer Utopia." In *A Critical Inquiry into Queer Utopias,* edited by Angela Jones, 231–44. New York: Palgrave Macmillan. DOI: 10.1057/9781137311979_10.

Warner, Michael. 1993. "Introduction." In *Fear of a Queer Planet: Queer Politics and Social Theory,* edited by Michael Warner, vii–xxxi. Minneapolis: University of Minnesota Press.

Wekker, Gloria. 1999. "'What's Identity Got to Do with It?' Rethinking Identity in Light of the Mati Work in Suriname."

In *Female Desires: Same-Sex Relations and Transgender Practices across Cultures,* edited by Evelyn Blackwood and Saskia Wieringa, 119–38. New York: Columbia University Press.

Weston, Kath. 1997. *Families We Choose: Lesbians, Gays, Kinship. Between Men – Between Women.* New York: Columbia University Press.

Wilkinson, Eleanor. 2010. "What's Queer about Non-monogamy Now?" In *Understanding Non-Monogamies,* edited by Meg Barker and Darren Langdridge, 255–66. Abingdon: Routledge.

Wittig, Monique. 1980. "The Straight Mind." *Feminist Issues* 1 (March): 103–11. DOI: 10.1007/BF02685561.

Yates, Luke. 2015. "Rethinking Prefiguration: Alternatives, Micropolitics and Goals in Social Movements." *Social Movement Studies* 14, no. 1: 1–21. DOI: 10.1080/14742837.2013.870883.